Rites of Shadow

E. A. St George

This is a revised and extended edition of material
originally published
in 1972 by Rigel Press as *The Devil's Prayerbook*.
Rites of Shadow © Elizabeth St George 2000

Revised and expanded version published by
ignotus press and Corvus Books 2000
BCM-Writer, London WC1N 3XX
Reprint 2002

British Library Cataloguing in Publication Data
ISBN: 0 9522689 7 3

Printed in Great Britain by
A2 Reprographics, Carmarthen
Set in Baskerville Old Face 11pt

Table of Contents

Foreword

Modern Witchcraft is - or should be - a pagan form of worshipping nature and the Goddess. This can be done individually or in a group, which is usually called a coven. Followers range from 'true believers' who are carrying on age-old traditions to fakers and exploiters who are after a quick buck or sexual gratification. It is the latter that have given Witchcraft such a bad name - with the help of the Sunday tabloids and other muckrakers who tar all Witches and pagans with the same brush.

It must be admitted that the popular image of Witchcraft is sometimes justified, though this really applies to people who are misusing it. Some coven leaders hold on to their followers using awe and apprehension. Should the follower desire to leave the coven, fear of 'occult reprisal' is used. This is a difficult fear to remove and some coven leaders have much psychological distress to answer for - their form of 'witchcraft' is both dangerous and harmful.

It is partly to correct popular misconceptions about Witches stemming from those who know little about the Craft that this book has been written. One hopes that it will provide useful information about the structure, practices and ceremonies of the Craft.

E.S.G

[In modern 'Wicca' it has become the norm for the festivals of the year to be designated by their Celtic names; this is not necessarily the case in Traditional Witchcraft. Many old-time Witches worked a 'double-blind' by using the names the Church had imposed over the older festivals, thus keeping their own allegiances hidden to the casual eavesdropper. What you choose to call your own festivals is up to you, but the author remains true to the Traditional way.]

Introduction

In 1999, Christine Sempers carried out an interview with Elizabeth St George for the Spring Equinox issue of *Alphard* magazine

The Magical Quilt-Maker

Elizabeth St George is an occultist of many years standing who has written books on a wide variety of magical subjects, both fiction and non-fiction, including *Basic Magic Spells, Magical Purification* and a *Guide to the Gods of Ancient Egypt*. She has also written for *Prediction* magazine.

She has several books of poetry and prayers to her credit including *Songs of Sorcery* and *The Dream Tree,* which are suitable for followers of many different pagan and occult Paths. What is unique about her and her writing, is a wonderful sense of humour and accessibility — so first of all, does she think a sense of humour is necessary in magical practice?

"Many occult writers take themselves far too seriously. They forget that laughter is an essential part of life, even in the occult."

Many years ago, the 'Powers that Be' asked her to consecrate a Prime Minister. The following day she had to deal with a small life-hunting entity in Birmingham. Obviously a sense of proportion is also a necessary ingredient. "One day I was masquerading in front of the world's press and the next day it was bucket and mop.

"If you think about it, some of the small jobs can be the most important ones in the long run. Consider feeding a baby shark; tomorrow it will return and want more food. It won't stay a baby for very long and one day it will return — with a lot of other hungry sharks.

"The same thing is true of astral entities who want blood. Give them a frog one day and they'll want two more tomorrow, plus a rabbit or a dog by the weekend. Blood sacrifice can get out of hand. Take a long hard look at Belsen. That's how an astral feeding frenzy can end. An astral bucket and mop can save the world!"

Many present-day writers seem to take themselves extremely seriously and yet her books have a definite sense of fun and, perhaps, a recognition of the absurdity of life and magic.

"You *have* to retain a sense of humour when you're working in the occult—it keeps things in perspective. Go back and consider the Kipling poem *If*... it doesn't matter if you walk with crowds or talk with kings. I've done both. It matters *more* to me that I do the best occult work that I can. I need to keep things in perspective. I need to laugh. We all need some laughter."

Over the years she's travelled the world and contact with other cultures has obviously influenced her magical development and perspective. "Yes, I have travelled widely and I've lived abroad, too. When I was a child, living in the West Indies, my grandmother and I found a cave with a voodoo altar set up. I suppose that taught me that not all worship is conducted in churches. It was obvious that you could conduct a service in a cave or some other place.

"The cave wasn't particularly big, so you couldn't have had a large gathering of people. I vaguely remember a statue of a sea goddess there — so obviously not everyone worshipped Jesus because the people who used the cave worshipped a sea goddess.

"The cave was on the sea shore; the worshippers may have been local fishermen, but it probably made a bigger impression on me than anyone realised. It demonstrated that there were other ways of doing things, and later on I learned about those ways."

Magicians are a secretive lot, so was it easy to make contact with practitioners in other lands, or was it simply a more every-day part of normal life? "Personally, I have never experienced difficulties

in contacting magical practitioners in other countries. I was in Iceland (would you believe I was doing astronaut training?), and I wanted to meet the High Priest of Iceland. I strolled into the lobby of the hotel and just asked the desk to get me the High Priest's telephone number.

"They did, and half an hour later, he came over. We had a couple of drinks and discussed the pagan world in Iceland. I think he blessed the hotel when he finally departed. It was a fascinating evening and it demonstrates that even telephones can turn into magical devices at times."

Over the years she must have seen a dramatic change in public attitude where the occult and its practitioners are concerned? "There certainly *have* been changes where magic and the occult are concerned. How much of that change is good or permanent is still uncertain. We're coming up to the New Age — that magic year 2,000. Many people are hoping for a more spiritual life-style. Plenty are hoping for a new Messiah, or the return of Christ but others are examining 'New Age beliefs'.

"That's fair enough, but by the year 2005AD, the New Age will be a distant memory. Less permanent stuff will be left behind — a vague recollection of New Age incense perhaps, but the rest will probably be considered passé as the next fad moves to centre stage. Like I said, the change of attitude may not be permanent."

Has she ever found a need to keep her own beliefs and practices private? "From my *own* personal point of view, I have lived in the same house for a long time. In all honesty, a lot of people did regard me with suspicion at first. Perhaps they'd read that Witches ate babies, or sacrificed cats, or some other idiocy printed in the Sunday papers.

"Well, we haven't had any neighbourhood babies missing and my neighbours know of my work with the animal kingdom. I hope that no one bothers to get horrified when I pass them in the road ... I think local people who know me would trust me absolutely.

They'd ignore foolish newspaper stories because they'd know better.

"Some years back, a disturbed teenager became obsessed with the number 666 and daubed a lot of graffiti on the local church wall involving that number. I know that the teenager blamed me for it, but the local vicar made him clean it up. The vicar *knew* who was responsible — he looked after his church as I look after my temple."

One of the books she published was called *The Necronomicon*, although there are several books of this title in print, and the name is much associated with the fantasy writings of H P Lovecraft. Why did she use that title when *The Necronomicon* has such an 'evil' reputation?

"*The Necronomicon* I published dates back to the time when I was doing a lot of travelling. I spent some time in South America with Madam Ruzo and her husband who collected ancient manuscripts, many of which were fascinating. Unfortunately I had limited time, but this particular manuscript held my attention. Consider Lovecraft's *Necronomicon* and those lines: *That is not dead which shall eternal lie,/And in strange aeons, even death may die*

"The writer of the Ruzo manuscript had exactly the same idea when he states of a mummy in a tomb: *They are not dead, unto the time that death itself is vanished.* It is exactly the same idea. I wonder if Lovecraft had seen a translation of the Ruzo document. It would certainly fit Lovecraft's description.

"Some of the spells in my publication would rank as murky magic, but a 10th century Arabian magician would have had rather different ethics. I've long since lost track of the Ruzo family but I'm glad I published the translation of their old manuscript. If this is the *real Necronomicon,* let's put it on record."

Of all the titles she's published over the years, does she have a favourite? "My personal favourite I suppose, must be *Voyage to*

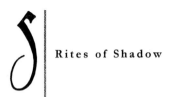

the Cat Star. I wanted to get a lot of mysticism into the story, along with a lot of colour. I wanted to time-plan the story from ancient Egypt to the far future and chart the course of a soul who was following her own path. *Voyage* seemed to work quite well."

With so much diversity in her writing, how would she define or describe her own magical Path? "My own magical work is strictly Qabalistic. I started by getting a job at the Atlantis Bookshop and learning the basics of occultism from the books which surrounded me. This was an extremely valuable experience because the occult is like a patchwork quilt with a lot of different patches (the green of Craft, the yellow of Healing; the blue of High Magic, and so on)."

And does the Master appear when the student is ready? "When my teacher walked in, I had a good basic grounding. I knew the vocabulary and we could build on the basics.

"I've often had students who wanted me to teach them magic in a week or some such request. I've referred them sharply back to their local library. They have to know their basics. They have to study the quilt. They can't be instant Adepts — the system doesn't work that way. I developed the courses I've written with this in mind. Rushing off and joining a magical group is *not* the right answer. It can turn into a disaster if you join the wrong one. Speaking the same language as your teacher and knowing the basics is much more likely to help both student *and* teacher."

Would she tell us the story behind *The Devil's Prayerbook.* How did she feel about the invocations and rituals which she'd composed becoming an accepted part of Traditional Wiccan worship?

"Ah, yes — *The Devil's Prayerbook.* Briefly what happened was as follows: I was preparing *Casebook of a Working Occultist* for publication. My publisher started talking of a wonderful magical manuscript called *The Devil's Prayerbook.* I ignored this until the secretary mentioned that the *Prayerbook* was written by someone with an identical name to my husband's and contained material about animal sacrifice. This suggested that *I* would be blamed for a book encouraging animal sacrifice — no way!

When I saw the manuscript, I noticed that many passages had been culled from other books: all presumably still in copyright. I pointed out to my publisher that he could not possibly publish the manuscript as it was because of the copyright law.

"As a result, he gave me a week to come up with a manuscript which could be published as *The Devil's Prayerbook*. I felt it was my obligation to keep the public out of trouble — but I felt bound to keep the Craft secrets that I knew.

"I also felt bound to keep my publisher out of the law courts. As I said, I was given one week in which to come up with a new manuscript and save the world from animal or baby sacrifice. That was how the book came to be written.

"That some of the *Prayerbook* has passed into coven practice is pleasing to me. If some foolish student tries to work from it, it won't harm him. If other people with power want to use the chants, that's great. I thought that perhaps I should hear them again in a subsequent incarnation and think that they sounded oddly familiar — and this has happened during a visit to Boscastle where they are part of the sound-track playing in The Witchcraft Museum!

"Meanwhile, I admit to being most amused when a newspaper published a comment about 'that quaint and curious book, *The Devil's Prayerbook* which came from ancient Egypt' ... really? I swear it came from my own typewriter. It's a real Elizabethan piece of work!"

As a result of this interview, we asked the author if she would be willing to up-date the typescript of *The Devil's Prayerbook* for re-publication under a less sensational title.

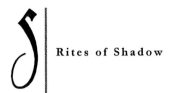

The Way Things Were

Witchcraft arose from a worship of nature and study of plant lore. It required considerable experience to handle many of the recipes associated with the Witches. Many plants are poisonous and some of the traditional mixtures are bizarre, but in ancient times plants were the only medicines available, and Witch-knowledge was not for the idle meddler.

The Wise Ones of old had very little in common with the modern Witch of today. They were frequently solitary workers who could not take long journeys each month at full moon to celebrate rites to the Goddess or the Horned God. The idea of a nude Witch is not traditional to this country; it is an idea imported from a warmer climate, though in some covens today it is exploited entirely for its sexual overtones. The English climate is not conductive to naked rompings in the dark, even in the warmest days of summer. Moreover, in all the surviving records of our Witchcraft trials, nobody was ever accused of working naked: surely it would have been noted down if they had!

Witches dancing around in a magic circle is a traditional picture, but the idea of a Witch performing a traditional ritual from a manuscript is not quite correct. The practices were never written down, partly for reasons of secrecy and partly because the majority of people could not read or write. High ceremonial magic requires exact working to a given formula, but most covens had their own formulae; they did not write the formulae down because they knew them by heart. At one point in our history it would have been dangerous to have a book of Witchcraft in your house. It might have cost you your life, and the lives of others dear to you.

Today members of the coven write down their traditions in a *Book of Shadows*. Some of the rituals enacted by the coven I was with were strictly Ceremonial Magic. In some cases the rituals were poorly rehearsed and badly done. This is ignorance in the extreme and very dangerous. Rehearsals *are* necessary. You build up your skills as you go along. Nobody becomes Head Witch in a week: it takes time and rehearsal. Like professional theatre, Witchcraft will not be alright on the night. You have to do the rehearsals before you achieve a great performance.

Some of the practices mentioned in some *Book of Shadows*, such as ritual scourging, are questionable. Ritual scourging is not native to this country. Indeed, scourging derives from the Christian sects, the Flagellates of the Middle Ages. Today it is sometimes used to cover a wild indulgence in flagellation. The scourge with its eight thongs and five knots in each tail, when used as a punishment tool, usually called for by the High Priestess for some misdemeanour, can be very painful.

The sexual angle

The coven which I joined claimed that the use of a scourge made the blood move faster to encourage the raising of power. That was not all that it raised. The sight of an elderly man flogging a naked, kneeling, bound young woman is sexually stimulating, and so is the reverse with its implication of sexual domination and submission. It is, moreover, illegal. Too much could go wrong at a flogging. The victim could end up in hospital, or dead. I would not recommend anyone joining such a coven.

The presentation of the working tools, especially the athamé and the white handled knife, is another example of sexual involvement. It is done by pressing the tools against the breasts of a woman who then presses herself against a man. On more than one occasion this gave rise to sexual excitement. Indeed, once the five-fold salute was given in such a way that it was unmistakeably cunnilingus and fellatio, nor was there any attempt to stop this - indeed everybody seemed to find it very amusing. However, later the same evening, the couple were privately interviewed and censured; as a result they left shortly after to set up their own group.

This particular event occurred when rivalry between covens had reached a new height and the amount of sheer bitchiness was incredible. From time to time this situation arises and can only be likened to petulant children claiming incredible abilities for their own gangs. After a few months peace feelers would be put out, and eventually all would be friends again.

The Great Rite or Third Degree, because of its sexual involvement, is frequently abused. It can certainly be harmful, or downright dangerous. There are many variations in the Sex-in-Magic but it is supposed that, at the moment of orgasm, the psychic senses and abilities of the individual can be heightened. Experiments in prolonging these moments are legion - and not just in magic. This is fine if the male and female can be matched with some sort of equality.

In practice, ages in coven members fall somewhere between eighteen and the late fifties or more. The mating of an old man with a young girl, or a young man with an old woman, is not always a delicate experiment, nor does it always take notice of 'sympathetic fertility'. With the decision of the High Priestess as final in the selection of the celebrants, I am convinced that there has often been more than just the ritual in mind when the choice is made.

Then there is the physical side to be considered. The choice of *coitus interruptus* or the complete act is left up to the celebrants. To the best of my belief, no one really knew what went on behind locked doors, but the excitement of those involved was certainly apparent. There were no virgins in the coven of which I was a member.

In so-called 'black' covens there may have been witnessed sex, perhaps in group form, but rumour is my guide and most covens do not go beyond the bounds of normal decency.

I want to mention a warning story at this point. A young woman at a disco voiced her desire to join a coven. A stranger overheard her remark and said that he would arrange this for her. All she needed to do was to turn up at a certain address the following evening. The young woman did, although the house appeared to be empty. She was admitted, blindfolded, beaten and raped. Whilst blindfolded, a number of flashes occurred. Two days later her father received a demand for money in return for the photographs.

NEVER trust a complete stranger where joining a coven is concerned. Any coven will want to meet you first, and you may have to undergo a period of probation before you are permitted to join. They want to know that you are reliable, sensible and sincere. Tensions can run high in any occult group. The leader or leaders don't want to invite you into their group if you're going to cause trouble. They've probably enough trouble on their hands already.

The young lady mentioned above was a victim of a sexual opportunist. I assume that he had access to an empty house and that he staged a 'fun' evening for himself and his friends. I know of a number a similar occurrences. They have a great deal to do with sex and nothing at all to do with real Witchcraft. Be prepared to wait before joining a real Craft coven.

Joining a Coven

With all these activities going on and the rumours that reach the outside world from time to time (usually through the Sunday tabloids), many covens get a lot of applications for membership. Applicants come from all walks of life and they are people of all ages. In responsible covens all applications are considered, but some are rejected because they just want to indulge in sexual power-games, people with certain medical conditions, those who have no idea what the Craft is about, or are too young.

Plenty of sexual deviants apply but few get further than the first interview. Those with medical conditions are not allowed either since the excitement and activities are not conducive to long life with a bad heart or some other medical infirmity. Those with little idea of what Witchcraft is about often write quite intelligent first letters, but reveal their lack of knowledge at their initial interview.

It is the young who cause the most headaches. Because of the tremendous psychological and sexual involvement, the young should be discouraged from joining a coven, but in many cases they are not. My own coven had an age limit of seventeen, and to give them credit, they held to it steadfastly. Other covens did not.

There are groups that snap up young people as they come along. Others lead them on until such time as they appreciate what is going on and have little chance to change their minds. Some time ago at a meeting of people to question Witches about the Craft, I counted fifteen young people present. Most of their questions were serious, but the answers invited more interest and an open invitation to come and witness a ritual was accepted with alacrity.

From here there is only one step further to go and that is to join. That is relatively easy. To get out is difficult. The young do not realise how hard it can be. They are made welcome at a time when they cannot appreciate the moral and spiritual dangers involved, but the same goes for many adults who join under the same circumstances. It's easy to get in and very, very difficult to get out.

The pressures put on members can be seen from some of the Initiation Ceremonies. Remember, they do not know what it is they are going in for, but they are impressed with the 'taking of their measure', the oath of allegiance, and that 'may their weapons turn against them should they break this solemn oath'. Very shortly after this, they are given a *Book of Shadows* to copy out. In the chapter on Obedience it is stressed that you never question the demands made upon you.

All this within the first few weeks will impress the suggestible neophyte with an aura of mystery, strange powers, and the ability of senior coven members to inflict terrible vengeance on them. As time goes on these feelings grow, especially when the neophyte begins to doubt some of the practices. The first suggestion to the

High Priestess that you wish to rethink the whole idea is often met with a kindly talk over a cup of tea, rather like a naughty child being tolerantly reminded of its obligations. From this point on the member is watched, just to see how the land lies. Possibly a 'banishing ritual' is performed, or some other rite which will have an electrifying effect on wavering members. Ritual curses and invocations to gods to strike one down imply all manner of terrifying penalties. A departing member is carefully reminded of this consequence, and it keeps them silent as a rule.

The waverers left behind are confused with conflicting beliefs and emotions, and terrified as to the correct thing to do. They are trapped by their own beliefs which bring on panic and neuroses. No one can lift this depression, save, perhaps, by a form of exorcism, or by proving conclusively that there is nothing to be afraid of. The attempts to retrieve my copy of *The Book of Shadows when I left that coven* were many and ingenious. Information was relayed that the Banishing Ritual had been performed, together with all sorts of threats and curses to bring me to heel.

I had left the coven because my academic interest in the Craft was suffering. Nothing happened to prove that there was any special power inherent in the Craft or its followers. At the time there was a lot of trouble in the movement generally and the press were having a field day. I left the coven for good, along with a couple of others. I believe one of these, a young girl, was 'reclaimed' and experienced a little trouble. Last I heard, she was still a member of the group.

Witchcraft, Satanism and fundamentalists

A lot has happened in the years since I first joined the Witchcraft movement. There has been much written on the subject of Satanism, Witchcraft and child abuse. Let's clear this up, because some journalists have left the public very befogged on the whole subject.

Satanism and Witchcraft are two totally different sets of beliefs and practices. People from one belief do not usually mix with those of the other. It is like inviting a Moslem and a Hindu to dinner. They may both come from India but they don't eat the same food and they could end up screaming with rage at each other. This is a book concerning Witchcraft. To Witches, children are sacred: they represent the future. It was never a part of Craft practice to abuse children and I doubt whether it was part of any Satanic belief either.

Unfortunately there are people in this world called *fundamentalists*— and not just Christian fundamentalists, there are Muslim fundamentalists and others just as determined to convert everyone to their way of thinking. These people do not like the idea of:

pagan gatherings
Witchcraft
covens
occult
temples
anyone of another religious belief.

You may have met some of these people. They are very sincere in their beliefs and some of them are very dotty! They are determined to prove that Witches, occultists, magicians and so on are all evil. This is not true. Alas, the fundamentalist has made up his mind and he doesn't want to change it.

Back in 1990, some devout Christian came up with the idea of converting everyone to Christianity by the year 2000. The Jews promptly pointed out that it was not their year 2000. The Muslims pointed out that it wasn't their year 2000 either. A number of people decided that they ought to start by converting the pagans, Witches and so forth by the year 2000. Fortunately most of us decided to stay exactly as we were. True, it *is* our year 2000 and the start of our Age of Aquarius. I imagine that most of my Witch friends celebrated the millennium ... but convert? I doubt it.

I believe that the fundamentalists are more responsible than

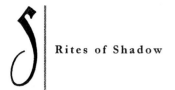

anyone for starting the rumours concerning 'Witchcraft and Satanic child abuse'. The newspapers played up these stories and the social services took them seriously, even taking children away from their homes in dawn raids. This reached the point of total idiocy in the Orkney Islands child abuse scare when one of the children accused an adult of dressing up as a Teenage Mutant Ninja Turtle and performing black magic and child abuse.

Let's clear this nonsense up. Turtles were not native animals to this country. Turtles have absolutely nothing to do with British Witchcraft. For some bizarre reason the Orkney Island social services may have *thought* that turtles were a symbol of Satanism and Witchcraft, but the social services got it wrong.

Early inhabitants of this island regarded themselves as 'People of the horse'. This animal was all-important, possibly because it represented the only available transport. The horse represented the most expensive purchase you were ever likely to make. You looked after your horse. You made sure it had food and shelter. Eating horsemeat was strictly taboo.

Today the car has replaced the horse. People feed their cars with petrol and try to shelter them in garages. The principle is exactly the same, and most of us still recoil from eating horsemeat! If we were looking for a totem animal today, many of us might pick the dog or cat because these have become our totem animals. Few of us have horses, but most of us have dogs or cats. I know of no occult group who have a turtle as an emblem!

We must expect children to read. We have universal education and most children do read. Sometimes they get hold of tabloid news-papers or books on magic and Witchcraft from the local library. I've met a number of young people who could paint 'magic signs' but it doesn't follow that they've been brainwashed by Witches. Some disused churches have been found to have 'magic signs' painted on the floor but it doesn't follow that *Witches* broke in and desecrated that church. Many Witches meet outdoors, usually in a forest where they are less likely to be seen. Others hold meetings in their own houses. Breaking into a disused church is not normal coven practice. I have never seen a Witch leaving a church with a can of paint and a guilty expression. The fundamentalists may accuse us of this sort of thing, but the Witches are not guilty.

Another abomination that surfaced in the 1990s was horse mutilation. Once again the press pointed its finger at the Witches. This is exceedingly unlikely. I have several Witch-friends who raise money for horse charities and many Witches sit on committees for animal charities. If the horse mutilation mystery is ever solved, I doubt whether any Witch will be found to have been involved. The tabloid press have a lot to answer for when it comes to putting the blame on the Craft.

One of the problems with Witchcraft/magic/the occult or whatever, is that it can provide a very useful cover story for non-witches who may be up to something else. Magic, for example, has links with the intelligence services. Back in the time of Elizabeth I the magician was a convenient cover story for a very skilful spy. He went to a number of European countries and courts as Doctor Dee, the famous magician. He also signed his letters as 007! Today's spy would not admit that he was putting microdots into a dead-letter box in an oak tree. His cover story might well be that he is a herbalist in search of mandrake, or that he meditates by moonlight. Not everyone who claims to be a Witch or a magician has anything to do with the Craft.

Drugs and similar substances

Yet another feature with a strong element of danger is the use of aromatics, drugs, decoctions and ointments in some covens. Providing these are carefully used under controlled conditions, there may be little harm in their application. Unfortunately they are seldom so controlled and some traditional recipes would certainly contravene the Poisons Act.

Decoctions of various plants to aid certain abilities are frequently employed without fully understanding their use. Sometimes there is a qualified practitioner on hand to give advice, but many covens experiment without proper preparation and without the materials to hand for first aid, if necessary. For example, patchouli correctly applied can aid psychic tendencies and meditation. Taken internally, it is highly dangerous.

The foxglove yields digitalis. The poppy produces opium. Both drugs are dangerous if wrongly used. What if vervain or any other plant or herb is used indiscriminately? Perfumes and incenses are used to create an atmosphere, but they can have hallucinatory effects. The idea behind their use is to separate the mind and body from everyday noises and influences. Incenses should aid you to concentrate on the magic in hand but few covens have a Witch who can render first aid. I was present when one coven member fainted but fortunately qualified help was available that evening. What happens when no help is on hand?

How do you convince someone that they should stick to a limited dosage? A member of the public rang me one night. She wanted an emergency purification bath. I suggested that she got a small bottle of peppermint oil from her local health shop. I told her to put five drops of the oil into the water: no more. This would make a basic purification bath.

The following day she rang me to complain that everyone's eyes were watering and that all her family had splitting headaches. How much oil did she use? "I reckoned that if five drops of peppermint oil would do me good, the rest of the bottle would be even better," she replied, "But then I didn't think you knew what you were talking about."

Doctors get the same problems with some patients who say, "I thought that two pills wouldn't work so I took the rest of the bottle ..." It can get very difficult when dealing with patients like that.

A Witch has to know the Poisons List and the Dangerous Drugs Act. Long ago pennyroyal oil was used to cause abortions.

Women do get raped and some fall pregnant as a result. Abortion was strictly illegal but the local Witch would be more sympathetic and reach for the pennyroyal. Otherwise back-street abortionists moved in to comfort and cash in on these unhappy women. Finally the government realised that abortions would take place anyway, therefore the operations had best be performed by doctors. Ask a Witch today for oil of pennyroyal and she will refer you to your medical practitioner. Ask a Witch for bluestone and you might be given 3 grams of copper sulphate. That's all. Copper sulphate is a poison. 3 grams in a bath won't hurt you but no Witch will provide you with a large jar of the stuff.

Ask a Witch for a 'loaded nutmeg' and he, or she, might prepare one for you. The nutmeg is supposed to be loaded with mercury and that is a poison. A practitioner might prepare one for you, but you would probably need a magnifying glass to see the bead of mercury inside. Witches are law-abiding, sensible people; we have no desire to poison anyone.

Analysis of the psychological side is less easy. An experienced Witch gains a lot of experience with such people. Some can be helped but I have met some who, I suspect, would be better off in padded cells. I have come across cases where curses were involved. I have also come across cases where illegal drugs have knocked the user right out of this reality. With the availability of such substances on the increase, it can become difficult to spot the fine line between curses and illegal drugs.

Witchcraft and fear

It is not easy to walk away from a Witchcraft coven, or any other occult group. For those who suffer the fears of a vengeful coven, their terrors can increase a hundred-fold. If the victim has a little knowledge, this can be a dangerous thing, for it creates all sorts of fears. The knowledge of evil is recognised but the fear of the Witch or the coven becomes so deep that nothing can remove it.

The correct treatment by experts takes a long time. The full implication of what magic and Witchcraft are can disturb the

psyche and even lead to insanity. The physical body suffers during the mental conflict for peace of mind.

On the other hand, fear has its uses. I have been present on several occasions when villainous people have found themselves in a coven of Witches and their lives have been 'turned around' by this unexpected encounter with the occult. One tiresome drug dealer spent the whole night talking to the Archangel Gabriel and confessing his many sins. He gave up his career as a dealer and now lives a clean and useful life, even taking his mother to church on Sundays. At times fear can be a very useful weapon in the hands of a Witch.

However, many people do react to the Craft and its Witches with panic. What I can say to those people - and those who want to experiment in Witchcraft - is this. Read about it, but never ever lose your common sense. Meditate, but spend the last minute of your meditation looking at a shoe, or a stone or something that signifies EARTH to you. Don't join a coven when a stranger offers to initiate you tomorrow night. Any self-respecting coven will want to know a bit about you before you join. Think COMMON SENSE!

Many Witches have very little power but many use psychology to inflict heartache and misery on those in their clutches. Consider a few facts that have hitherto been taken for granted. Neophytes have been told that the secrets of Witches may never be revealed. Why, then, do Witches permit those little excursions of writers and the press into their covens? Why do they give away snippets of information here and there to titillate the credulous? Why do they allow parts of their *Book of Shadows* to be published? Why do they allow some of the rituals on television and appear to explain the meaning behind some of their activities? What punishments are meted out to the press, the interviewer or the betrayer? (Punishment, remember, is contradictory with the requirements of the Craft.)

Nothing. Why, then, should the rank and file Craft member be 'leaned upon' not to do as they themselves are doing?

When dealing with Witches, much goes unexplained and unanswered. It is expected that orders will be followed blindly, as regrettably they often are. Now, perhaps, the Witches can be dealt with on their own ground. Let us take away the veneer of secrecy and show the sort of practice that goes on.

The Book of Shadows

To my mind, it was simply a matter of time before a complete *Book of Shadows* was put before the general public, perhaps by a sympathiser with the Craft. I started by being a sympathiser but became a doubter. After many years in the wilderness, I have to admit to a certain sympathy again.

The Book of Shadows that forms the second part of this book claimed to be a collection of writings handed down for many years. Some may detect its true origin, for it gives the impression of being far more recent. It has never been published before in this form, as copied from a master copy by a coven member, although recently large chunks of it are to be found, differing slightly in wording, in several books on the Craft.

A BRIEF LOOK AT THE MODERN WITCH

The modern Witch follows the old religion of the Wicca, 'Wicca' meaning the wise, or wise people. It is a faith involving sympathetic magic and fertility and it is often dominated by the female. True, there are male Witches, often called 'warlocks although this is a relatively modern term. The focal point of worship is primarily the Goddess of the Moon, but a mixed coven of today would work with the Horned God as well as the Moon Goddess.

Witchcraft, Wicca, the Way of the Wise, has nothing to do with Ceremonial, Ritual or 'black' magic. It does have its own rites and rituals, although in these you will find nothing of the reported sacrifices, sexual deviations or black cocks and white hens being destroyed and their blood being poured over the body of a naked woman (the last-mentioned being a voodoo spell).

Some Witches work naked, but this is entirely optional. Some covens use special robes. One Witch, working out of doors, even uses consecrated gumboots. Most covens who brave the vagaries of the British weather make do with their members dressed alike in a plain white or black shift. No, not because they are practising 'black' magic but for a very practical reason: We live in a twenty-four hour civilisation today. If you wish to pass unseen through the darkness, then you will probably dress in black and hope that the local reporter is asleep, along with everyone else. Black cloaks are very practical if you're trying to walk to a blasted heath at night.

The normal coven should consist of thirteen people when holding a ceremony, although there may be twenty or thirty people who belong to the coven. With today's requirements in business etc., it is not always possible to attend monthly meetings or the festivals throughout the year. Some covens celebrate their meetings at full moon since that was the safest night for travelling before street lights came along. Other covens celebrate at new moon. Today most coven meetings take place on the nearest Saturday night when the moon is waxing, never waning.

Extra to the thirteen meetings, or inclusive, are the following celebrations from January to December:

January - New or full of the Moon
February - Candlemas, new or full of the moon.
March - Vernal Equinox and new or full of the moon.
April - Walpurgis Night and new or full of the moon.
May - New or full of the moon
June - Midsummer Eve, Summer Solstice meeting
July - New or full of the moon
August - Lammas or New or full of the moon
September - Autumn Equinox, or new or full of the moon
October - Samhain or Hallowe'en
November - New or full of the moon
December - Winter Solstice, new or full of the Moon

These are the regular meeting nights of the year. Many covens meet every Saturday night to install neophytes or deal with requests from outsiders. Moreover, as it is their religion, they receive some pleasure from holding a religious meeting.

The Coven hierarchy is governed by the High Priestess and her deputy-partner, the High Priest, who ranks second in command. The High Priest usually interviews would-be initiates whilst the women deal with their own sex. Also of prime importance in to-day's covens are the Astrologer, the Herbalist and the Teachers of the Craft. These would be members most adept in the sciences, the history of the Wicca and those well up on ritual invocations.

Witchcraft degrees

There are three degrees in Witchcraft. The first degree is the initiate, the newcomer. Some people never get beyond this level; it may be that they do not want to go any further. This is permissible,

for in the established church not everyone takes up the priesthood. In the Craft, so long as they are content, no one questions their decision.

The second degree is that of the High Priestess or High Priest. These are the experienced people of the Craft, those who have trained to be the Astrologer or Herbalist, Diviner or Lore Teacher. After twelve months they are raised to the higher degree and then, following further training, they begin instructing the new members. After attaining the second degree, they may even form their own coven. It is not permitted for a first degree Witch to form a coven, though in practice a High Priestess may allow an initiate to perform a ceremony with prompting, if and when necessary, much as a theatre prompter might assist an actor.

The ritual for attaining the Third Degree has never been written down in any *Book of Shadows*. It is deliberately omitted and rarely mentioned. When a Third Degree ritual is performed, no initiate or outsider is present. Generally the Third Degree is carried out at the New Moon and, of course, away from the normal monthly meetings. Occasionally other covens may be invited along for the evening. Afterwards there is usually quite a celebration. Senior members of both covens may take this opportunity to develop policy concerning the outside world, plan a new coven or discuss research and achievements since the last meeting of such a nature.

Sometimes there is a Grand Coven meeting where all present are Third Degree Witches and therefore any rituals or magic performed should be exceptionally effective. Third Degree Witchcraft is often referred to as the Great Rite, and as the ritual is concerned with sex, it is here that the wild stories of perversion and sexual debasement have their origins. There is little truth in these stories. Most of them are fabricated by the tabloid newspapers to increase their circulation figures. The sexual part is optional but it may take place behind closed doors with nobody present except the celebrants.

Some further defence against these stories must be made.

During any ordinary party as the evening wears on and the smoke hangs heavy in the air, couples pair off for petting. It's often the best part of the party. This may well take place after some Craft ceremonies, although there are definitely no orgies in more sincere circles. Some horseplay may occur, but amusement is the prime mover, not sex.

Photographs are rarely taken. During my coven membership there were visits from the Press and magazine photographers, but no one blackmailed any prominent person in a compromising position. Even at a Witch Wedding, the only sexual involvement was the five-fold kiss and a quick embrace with a token normal kiss..

The Craft as Religion

The Craft and its members make a religion in spite of everything. The Witches are frowned on by the Established church, feared by the ignorant, persecuted by many and desired by the lustful. The Craft has a history of persecution but it survives because of the loyalty of a few strong followers. Their zeal and fervour endure, despite the nasty stories.

I was present at an attempt to seek out a very nasty murderer. The press account of this stated that thirty thousand Witches were coming to one ordinary house to brew up a potion to catch the murderer. I don't know where they got their story from but it certainly had nothing to do with what happened at that meeting. Their account was pure fiction. And yes, the murderer *was* caught two days later. I would have to say that the working had been very successful, despite the Press account.

Tales of young children being involved in Witchcraft are mainly untrue. Children belonging to coven members may be instructed in the religious aspects of the Craft. They may be allowed to stay up for a bonfire at Hallowe'en. They might even be allowed their ration of 'Blood soup and dead men's fingers' (tomato soup and sausages) but then into bed before the adults' party gets started. No one under eighteen is allowed into a reputable coven's gathering.

Tales of animal sacrifice are also untrue. Such a business brings

with it a serious *magical* danger which most of us would prefer to avoid. A National newspaper who should have known better recently printed an article linking missing cats to Witch initiations. This is total nonsense. A few years back, West London suffered thirty thousand missing cats. It had nothing to do with Witchcraft but it did have a great deal to do with the fur trade. I regret to add that the German fur trade liked British cat pelts because the animals were well fed and in good condition. I can also assure readers that the men behind this racket had a great many curses hurled at them.

Regardless of what the tabloids say, Witches are pretty nice people and they do their best.

Interviewing would-be members for a coven is done in secrecy, not only for the sake of coven members, but also for the sake of the aspirant. Do not be surprised if you are put on probation for a while. But, with the publication of these rituals and nothing held back, membership may even increase, once would-be Witches know what they're in for! The sincere person will, if accepted by a good coven, be taught much. He (or she) will benefit from a deeper spiritual purpose and be the richer for it. The frivolous person and the dabbler should stay away, for the Way of the Wise is not for them.

MATERIALS OF THE CRAFT

Like her forerunners, the modern Witch uses mystic diagrams and tools, herbs, rare liquids and brews, incantations and rituals to further the religious aspect of life. Today she may also use a computer for astrology and numerology. She seldom performs any unusual activities outside her magic circle, for this is her protection if she makes a mistake.

Many years back, during the time of persecution, the Witches were in real danger at every meeting. If someone spotted Witches gathering every full moon on the local blasted heath, it would be easy for the authorities to arrest everyone in the coven. It became customary for the Witches to change the site of their meeting place every time. If they met by the lake for the January meeting, then they would meet in the woods for February and so on. This meant that a circle had to be drawn for the meeting and the ground inside the circle would be consecrated for the next few hours. At the end of the meeting, the circle would be banished and all equipment taken home. The less the hostile church authorities knew, the less likely the Witches would be persecuted. It is likely that coven members used masks and hoods on such occasions, just to make them more difficult to identify.

Today, the position is *slightly* different. Many Witches have, or aim to have, a room set aside in their house for the practice of the Craft. Those who have such rooms regard them as consecrated places. They are permanently set up for Witchcraft and there is no need to mark out a circle every time. Nor are the church authorities likely to break into your house and drag you away to torture you.

A permanent circle exists in a sixteenth century Hertfordshire cottage. Inside is a circle with symbols, whilst the walls are covered with occult inscriptions: all mod cons laid on. It is not the only such place where a circle or temple exists, but it may be the oldest site.

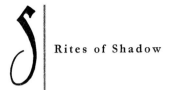

The Witch will perform her ritual in perfect safety at the right time within her circle or room. Usually the right time occurs during the hours of darkness. This is traditional. Before the age of electricity, people rose early and went to bed at sunset. If you wanted to hold a clandestine meeting, you did so during the hours of darkness when others were asleep. And if you were having a Witchcraft party, when do you usually hold a party? Most parties today are held in the evening or at night, during the hours of darkness.

The ceremonies are performed using the tools of the Witch's art which are mentioned in *The Book of Shadows*. These tools include the athamé, a black handled knife with an inscribed hilt or blade. There is also a matching white-handled knife. Both must have been consecrated in a circle by a High Priestess before they can effectively be used. A Witch may need a ceremonial sword. She will certainly need several small dishes of silver, a candlestick for the altar, and four other candlesticks to set at the cardinal points around the altar. Candles are very seldom black, in fact they are usually white, but some Witches use coloured candles that match the ritual. There should also be a small, metal plate, six inches (15 cm) across, inscribed with the pentagram.

Other tools are the wand, usually made of hazel and about fifteen inches long. There may also be a scourge, the symbolic flail of the Egyptians, which has eight thongs about twelve inches long, each thong being knotted five times.

Several cords will be needed: Red, white or silver, green or blue. Dressing gown cord is often used because it can be cut to the right length (4' 6" or 137 cm) and comes ready coloured from many department stores. Other materials needed during Craft rituals (cakes and wine etc.) are placed behind or beside the altar. Finally small quantities of salt water and olive oil are needed to complete the scene.

Requirements vary from coven to coven. Some covens insist that a woman's personal jewellery should be placed on the altar before each ceremony and returned after consecration. Witchcraft jewellery is almost always silver, for this is the metal of the moon and therefore used for necklets, rings, earrings or armbands. Sometimes there is a single garter worn as a badge of office by the High Priestess. The garter may be black, though I have seen other colours used as well, the traditional material being snakeskin. Males generally wear no insignia of any sort, although some Third Degree men will wear a silver band on their upper arm.

In today's world there is something of a fashion for magical jewellery, including the pentagram. This can be found on rings, pendants and all sorts of other jewellery. In days gone by, such items would have been unthinkable. If you were caught wearing a pentagram ring, the authorities would be certain that you had dealings with the devil. A bracelet with magical signs on it would bring the wearer a heap of trouble unless the signs were on the inside where no one could see them. The majority of country people were very poor, but even the poorest among them could afford a strand of silver wire to wear on her finger, symbolising that she worshipped the Moon Goddess.

Today 'magical' and Craft jewellery is on sale at New Age shops. Quite a few people now wear pentagram rings or pendants so do not assume that anyone wearing such jewellery is a Witch. I know of one young man who worried his potential father-in-law by wearing a pentagram ring. The older man assumed that this was a symbol of the CND! The youngster wasn't that way inclined, nor was he a Witch. The ring was simply a present.

Although the circle once formed should not be broken, a 'gateway' is left to be opened and closed by the High Priestess as necessary. The gateway is usually between South and West with the altar set East to West, backing to North. It has to be big enough to take the tools of the art and it should be waist high. Technically the altar should never be round, or oval, but it does rather depend on the most useful table to hand. Sometimes the altar is placed in the centre of the group, but in practice it is not always needed and it may be moved out of the way after the initial ceremony. When a coven meets indoors, it is advisable to have a changing room, and someone delegated to answer the door to unexpected visitors. Rituals should be worked by candlelight.

For an outdoor ceremony the altar is set in the North of the circle and the centre point of the working will be a small fire, enough to give off some heat but small enough for two people to leap over the flames without danger. Clothes, or lack of them, depend entirely on coven rules and British weather.

A symbolic cauldron is used when rituals are held out of doors. This dates back to days long gone when many people who attended Craft meetings spent most of their lives starving. At a Craft meeting, a rich man might bring a lamb for the feast and the poorest person could gather a few herbs for the cooking pot. Elderly people had problems with teeth, but a well-cooked stew meant that they could have a serious meal. Everyone had enough to eat at a Craft party. Today, the cauldron frequently serves as a soup kitchen or a stew pot during a break in the ceremonies.

Little statuettes of the Moon Goddess or the Horned God are often used as altar ornaments. The Goddess appears as Diana, most frequently cast in silver, although any metal except gold will do for her statue. The Horned God is frequently cast in bronze. You might even find appropriate statuettes in antique shops, junk stalls or car boot sales but these should be cleansed and re-consecrated before use.

You usually find an incense burner at one corner of the altar. Incense symbolises air in indoor ceremonies. Some covens use joss sticks. If they are bought, they are usually the Chinese variety, not the Indian ones. It is possible to make one's own joss sticks and incense can also be home-made from traditional recipes.

Amulets, charms, talismans and so on are also made at home, although silver charms are usually purchased from New Age shops or occult emporia. Cakes are baked by a coven member and a bottle of ordinary white wine is used for the cakes and wine ritual.

The size of the circle tends to vary from coven to coven. The original circle was 9' (275 cm) in diameter and marked out using the 4' 6" cord. Today's circles are often 11' (335 cm) in diameter with a 9' circle inside. It is not really necessary to add mystic inscriptions between the two circles but it does look terrific.

If you want to greet a Witch, here's how it's done: The regular greeting is "Blessed be" given with the sign of the Horned God. Contrary to popular belief, this is signalled by raising the little and fourth finger. The thumb covers the folded index and third finger. Within the coven the five-fold salute is given by kissing the feet, the knees, organs, breast and lips.

Scourging is also ritually symbolic as it is intended to purge the soul with light strokes *par derriere*, a practice not limited to the Witches Sabbat. It was also practised by penitents of Mother Church. Amongst the devout the scourge was applied indiscriminately, but in a coven the prescribed number of forty strokes is applied in a peculiar sequence, 3-5-8-11-13, with a pause in the grouping.

Here are the directions for tying the cords ritually: The practitioner holds his right wrist with his left behind his back. He is loosely bound with a cord that goes up around his neck and down to make a triangle. Another cord is placed around the neck to be used as a halter or lead. A last cord is bound about the top of the left thigh: this must not trail on the ground, otherwise brethren might trip up and go flying!

Now we are almost ready to start work.

A length of red thread and a blindfold should complete the normal requirements, and don't forget your small silver bell to sound before and after invocations.

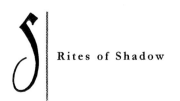

THE RIGHT TIMES, DAYS AND MATERIALS
Traditionally the days of the week are sacred to seven different powers

Sunday began as Sun-day, i.e. it was dedicated to the sun deity. Modern witches would regard it as a day of good things and a suitable day for healing ceremonies.

The sun governs the following vocations: Theatre, television and radio, film producers, executives, financiers, diplomats, healers. The gems and metals are diamond, carbuncle, chrysolite, gold and topaz. Its animals are the lion, the eagle, the cock, the condor, the ibis and the parrot. The following plants are sacred to the sun: Golden rod, golden glow, camomile, orrica, sunflower, scarlet sage, yellow roses, peppermint, lemon and tangerine plants, laurels, lavender, sage and thyme. The correct number for use in magic and invocations is 1 or 6, and the colour is golden yellow.

Monday began as Moon-day, i.e. it was dedicated to the ancient lunar goddess. The Moon Goddess dealt with women and children, dreams and divination. She can also deal with psychiatric illness. She is likely to be invoked when the moon is new, waxing or full. Working on the waning moon is not considered a good idea.

The moon covers the following careers: all aspects of work at sea, impersonators, inns and hotels and some of the farm and food industry. The sacred animals include shellfish, mosquitoes, bats, moths, rabbits and hares, the nightingale, snails, frogs, and cats. The jewels are moonstone, cat's eye, pearl, and crystal, all of which should be set in silver. Plants governed by the moon are olive and willow trees, melons, pumpkins, lily and lotus. The colour is silver or white. The number is 9.

Tuesday is associated with the War God. Few people actually want a war god but if you wanted to protect a soldier going into battle, then you might schedule a ritual for a Tuesday might. It might also be used for justice or to help someone going into hospital for surgery. Where justice is concerned, please remember that the justice of the gods doesn't always suit human beings and it might not suit you either.

The War God governs all the armed services, also engineers, dentists, chemists, harpoon and fireworks manufacturers, metal work, agitators, thieves, rogues and vagabonds (if these last three are vocations). The jewels and metals are bloodstone, garnet, ruby, jasper and iron. His animals include all creatures with stings and poisons, scorpions and venomous snakes, wasps, hornets and so on. Hawks, vultures, beasts of prey such as the jackal and the wolf come under this power. His plants are hops, capers, hemlock, thistles, leeks and onions, chives, hawthorn, heather, box wood and tamarisk. The number is 5 and the appropriate colour is red.

Wednesday is associated with Mercury. Mercury was the God in charge of transport. Today he looks after cars as well as chariots. Old statues show Mercury wearing winged sandals, thus he looks after airlines as well. This particular deity had a tremendous sense of humour, so remember that when your holiday flight is delayed. He also looks after computers, E-mail and the post office.

Mercury rules publishers, travel in all forms, travellers, scientists, street traders and lawyers. Jewels for this planet include carnelian, aquamarine, agate, mercury or fire opals. The sacred animals tend to be the fox, the monkey, the lynx, insects of all kinds, ants, the weasel, and the laughing hyena. The plants are hazelnut, the berry and ash trees, myrtle, clover and fern, burrs, celery, endive, madder, elder, parsley, thyme, caraway, arrowroot and lavender. Mercury magic belongs to Wednesday, so the right day is Wednesday. The colour is orange and the number is 8.

Thursday is associated with Jupiter. This is the deity who looks after the good things in life, good luck, benefits, charity money,

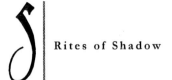

well-being. You could certainly call upon him before a party but be a careful that you don't spend too much money on the alcohol. Jupiter can be very generous with gin and people who indulge in 'one for the road' might not live to thank you.

Jupiter looks after government, the church, teachers, explorers, engineers, discoverers and officialdom in general. His jewels are the sapphire, lapis lazuli, amethyst, turquoise. His metal is tin. His animals are the crow, magpie, eagle, lion, deer, dogs, elephants, cows, oxen, buffaloes, horses and weasels. His plants include the blueberry, blackberries, eucalyptus, spinach, chicory, cloves, asparagus, anise, rose, cornflower, juniper, the horse chestnut, the chestnut, apricot and fig trees, quince, aloe, colchium and cedar. The number is 4 and the colour is blue.

Friday is associated with the Goddess of love magic. If you are attempting anything in the way of a love spell, this is the right day for such a ceremony. Remember that Venus is one emotional Goddess and that love can turn to hatred. If you are planning such a ritual, think very carefully about the wording of the love spell. You don't want two lovers killing each other.

Venus rules the fashion world, jewellers, cosmetics and all trades connected with the body. She also rules performers such as film and television actors, entertainers, music and the arts. Her jewels are emeralds, alabaster, opals, corals and white pearls. Her special metal is copper. Her animals are the butterfly, the bee, partridges, peacocks, household pets such as goldfish, dogs and cats etc., singing birds. Venus plants include the birch, cherry, plum and pear trees, violets, lilac, primula, poppies strawberries, gooseberries, artichokes, coriander, Easter daisy and periwinkle. Her number is 7 and her proper colour is green.

Saturday is associated with Saturn, the ancient God of Age and Time. A lot of people confuse Saturn with Satan and they jump to the conclusion that this is 'black' magic. This is not quite true. You could use Saturn's magic to bless an elderly person, to help a widow get through her dark times, to raise money for research into Alzheimer's disease or to run a happy retirement party. Satan wouldn't assist any of these projects but Saturn would assist you.

Saturn deals with research scientists, farm workers, mine owners, the lead and lumber industry, undertakers and associated professions, stone quarry workers, tannery and leather workers. Saturn's jewels are chalcedony, onyx, black coral, dark jade, sardonyx, malachite and jet. Saturn's metal is lead. The appropriate animals include beetles and crustaceans, moles, owls, beavers, pigs, bears, goats, the crane, the ostrich and the dinosaurs. The correct plants include the holly, mistletoe, ivy, evergreens, pansy, beet, hemp, beech, poplar and palm trees, quince, yew, red oak, weeping willow, mandragora, hemlock, moss, mugwort, and aconite. The number is either 3 or 8 and the colour for Saturn's magic is black.

Not everyone will agree with all the above-mentioned correspondences. These were taught to me by the coven of which I was a member. Other covens have other beliefs.

Imagine that you are about to take a swim in the sea. The tide can assist you or it can make it impossible for you to reach your target. There are magical tides that run through the days of the week. They can assist you with your ceremony, but if you take the wrong tide then it will be that much more difficult to achieve the desired result. Wait for the right tide if possible. The same is true of the materials. You don't want to make a love charm out of lead when it ought to be made of copper.

It is not always practical in this day and age to run ceremonies on their right days and hours. You cannot hope to run a love ceremony at 7 a.m. on a Friday morning if you have to get your family off to work before 8 a.m. Nor can you do a ceremony in your workplace, or while you are waiting for a bus. Most of us have to wait until late at night before we can begin such magical work. If you can time your ceremonies so that they occur on the right day/

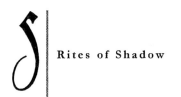

evening/night and you have time to concentrate without interruptions, then you should work successfully. Distraction in the middle of a spell can be a very serious matter for the person who is working. Small wonder that a lot of Witches keep rather late nights and turn off their mobile telephones.

You may petition the God and the Goddess for whatever you like, but always remember that they can say 'No'. Consider a newly qualified driver petitioning you for a red sports car. You know that he has only just got his licence and he hasn't got the experience to drive a sports car safely. You may feel inclined to grant that young person's wish but you would be wiser to get a sedate car for the young man and let him get road sense before he gets a sports car. Sometimes you have to remind petitioners that 'No' is also an answer, even if it isn't the answer they want to hear.

I once had a petitioner beg me to help her regain her husband's love. I had every sympathy for her until I took a long hard look at her Tarot cards; then I saw that her husband had put her in hospital twice, and the third time he would kill her. The finest magic I could offer her was help in packing her suitcase and leaving town. This was not the sort of help that she wanted, but it might have saved her life if she had listened to me.

Remember that the original God and Goddess were obliged to grant their worshippers only four things: A fireplace in a home of their own, food for the worshippers and their animals, flax for their backs and a friend with whom to share their lives. Those are the four basics, and I do mean basics. A fireplace in a home doesn't mean a palace. Food doesn't mean a five course dinner at the Savoy. Flax doesn't mean a fur coat and the sex of the friend is unspecified.

Any other item was a luxury. Sacks of gold and gems? They might be given to a petitioner - maybe. It depended on the wisdom of the deities. If the petitioner nagged too much, then the gold just might be dropped on the petitioner's head! I mention this because many people feel that money is the right answer to all their problems and they attempt to win huge sums from the lottery. Restrain yourself: you might end up with a heart attack as you go to collect the cash and it won't do you any good at all.

POT POURRI

It is not my intention to list in detail any particular formula or remedy involving herbs and plants. Some can be very dangerous. In the event of the reader wishing to experiment with old spells, please be careful. You might have a very unpleasant experience and you could do untold damage. You may or may not achieve your aim. You are sincerely advised to contact an expert in the field, for safety's sake ...

The following miscellany is collected at random from books and from Witches, and there are plenty more recipes where these came from:

"To have courage, pluck five teeth from the mouth of a live lion and you shall have no fear" (and make sure that the lion doesn't have you!).

"Be careful of mishandling parsley for you and yours suffer within the year." (Today, in some parts of the country, no one will herd parsley for fear of trouble ensuing for the picker or his family.)

"Scratch the name of your enemy upon lead using the pin feather of a live bald vulture which has dropped in the hour of Saturn." (Better ask London Zoo for some help on this one).

"Ignore the snowdrop and hurt its feelings and it will not grow the following year."

"Raspberry leaf tea can cure kidney problems."

Along similar lines are very old superstitions about abusing the following wild plants as they are considered to belong to the devil: stitchwort, plantain, sun sponge, shepherds needles, house-leek, yarrow, parsley, wild garlic, aconite, hemlock, ragwort and black-berries after 1st of October when the devil is presumed to have spat on them!

"If caught in a storm and you are near an elder tree, you may shelter beneath its branches safely." (There is an old superstition that the original Cross was made from the wood of an elder tree.)

"For jaundice, take the roots of ground ivy and boil in water for some time. Let the patient drink some of it to ease his suffering."

"If a Witch shake her hair loose of all encumbrance when making a curse, it will double the strength of the evil, but take a hair of a sleeping Witch and put it in the earth and you will nullify the curse."

"Rine is a plant that can be thrown at a faithless one to cure unfaithfulness. Clover can be used as an antidote to poison or to aid clearer vision. Rine leaves can be used to help in the cure of hydrophobia."

Witchcraft lore includes many other plants: Valerian is used to cure many ills, and shares with mistletoe the name of All Heal. It was and is still used in the cure of nervous disorder, insomnia, cough, etc. It has connections with being used as an aphrodisiac.

The violet has earned its place in the history books for love charms and philtres, and as a cure for ulcers. It is sometimes mixed in salads etc. Infusions of the flower and/or the leaves have been used to cure fevers, jaundice, pleurisy and colds. Adders tongue fern is used in lotions and salves for open sores and wounds, and the 'tea' of the leaves is used to help in purification of the blood.

Betony cures haemorrhages, insomnia and fatigue. It is also an aid against visions, bad dreams and drunkenness.

With today's stresses, it is not surprising that many people suffer from headaches. You have probably been through the range of proprietary medicines and found them wanting. As an alternative, you might do worse than try one of the following:

> Camomile tea or laying the head on a pillow
> stuffed with camomile leaves.

> Wear a violet wreath.

> Sage tea or elder tea, or boil chrysanthemum roots
> and drink the infusion when warm.

> Rub horseradish on the forehead or press mustard leaves against
> the forehead (keep both well away from your eyes).

> Bind the cast-off skin of a snake around the forehead
> and it will ease the pain.

Traditional Witches were supposed to use an ointment that would allow them to fly. All the recipes for this ointment that I have been able to trace require ingredients that are both illegal and dangerous. Look them up elsewhere if you must. But don't try them - you have been warned!

Witches also make talismans and charms, since people want charms for all sorts of things. There is no easy step-by-step guide for making all sorts of talismans; much thought and preparation is necessary. Buying a lucky piece by mail for a couple of pounds will not do for highly personal wants. You have to make the right thing of the right material using the proper tools. You ought to make it on the right planetary day and, preferably, at the right hour. Here is one example:

A talisman is required to assist a man to hold down his job as a salesman in the Wholesale Canned Goods Industry.

Analysis: The principal ruler here is Mercury with the Moon as a second though equally important factor. If you cannot afford a silver disc (and Mercury is liquid at normal temperature), then look to the woods ruled by Mercury and then the Moon. Hazel is the obvious choice. It must be fashioned into a suitable size, ready for inscription and design to be engraved upon it at the correct hour. (Much of the above is low magic and not strictly Witchcraft, but some Witches specialise in this sort of thing and it is therefore included.)

You will have to know the Qabalistic tables for each planet and their correct signs and sigils. The correct occult alphabet should also be used. The Divinatory Arts are not pure Witchcraft, although some of the little-used or unknown practices are regarded as such.

We have touched on Astrology but some Witches occasionally use palmistry, numerology, phrenology, graphology, physiognomy, cartomancy, dice and tea cup readings, etc. You don't have to join a coven to study these subjects but you do need the experience of an adept to guide you through the Craft.

The religious side of the Craft is reward enough to the disciples of the faith, but to have the fascination of these richly absorbing subjects in support makes, for them, the most rewarding part of their occult studies.

THE WITCH AND MONEY

There was a time, a long time ago, when the Witch did not handle money at all. The Witch had delivered the farmer's wife of a healthy infant and she could expect a generous supply of eggs, milk or butter. She had cured the tailor of an allergy and that was worth new clothing, and so on. There were no village shops and there was only a pedlar or chapman who came from miles away. The pedlar's pack carried all sorts of useful stuff. If someone had given the Witch a penny then she might buy a packet of pins, but that was about all she needed. She made herself into a successful Witch and she did very well without a large supply of cash.

The situation has changed today, so how much money are we talking about?

If you join a coven who use desktop publishing for the coven papers and rituals, then someone has to pay for the paper. You may be asked to put a few pounds in to cover the costs. Robes need replacing from time to time. If you are working in a coven which uses robes, someone will have to buy the material for those robes, even if they are sewn by a member of the coven. You will be asked to put in a few pounds to cover the costs. If you're planning a coven party, someone will have to buy the wine and you will be asked to contribute to the bill.

In practice, many covens keep a small fund of their own to deal with these expenses. It is usually supervised by the High Priest so that there are a few pounds in hand to meet the next problem, whatever it is. If you have your own Witchcraft room, then you will need cleaning products and a coat of paint. You may want suitable curtains and a carpet on the floor. Your basic equipment should not be expensive, and you keep that for the rest of your life. You can make your own robe.

Purely for the record, I have had an occult room for about forty years. It has had three coats of paint in that time, four sets of curtains and one carpet. I am inclined to buy rather plain robes, not fearfully expensive ones. This does not make for an expensive hobby. Plenty of people spend a great deal on their Saturday nights out. I don't.

It should be noted that local councils are not friendly when it comes to Witches. Sometimes they don't like the idea of changing the use of a bedroom into a Witchcraft room. The path of wisdom lies in keeping silent where officials are concerned. They might get worried by the truth. If the local council finds out that you are making and selling talismans and charms, they will do their best to stop you and close your business down. They probably wouldn't recognise a talisman or charm, but they'll tell you to stop it anyway!

How much should you pay for a charm or amulet or talisman? This depends on what YOU want to pay. If you want a simple written talisman, I suggest about £15.00. The witch has probably got all the materials in stock, but it will take time to make the product.

If you want a silver talisman, then you will have to pay for the silver. My guess would be £30-£50, but it depends on how much silver you want. If you want a spectacular hunk of silver jewellery, then the price might go higher.

If you want a gold talisman with ten carats of diamonds, then you must remember that diamonds work out at about £1,000 per carat and gold is also expensive, even before anyone starts work on turning these things into a talisman. [These figures are based on 1999 prices. I don't want anyone complaining in five years time that these figures are hopelessly out of date!]

There have been a number of changes in the occult world since I became a practitioner. There's now a New Age movement and many people are hoping to tune in on spiritual matters. However, there are two points I want to raise here. They are both confidence tricks which have come to my notice and they have caused concern.

For many years I did 'occult supply' work, turning out oils, incenses, bath salts and so on for a London shop. I could turn out a jar of bath salts for £2.00 and make a very modest profit. The shop would double that price to the customer. All right, the shopkeeper has his bills to pay, his assistants' wages and so on.

The day came when a petitioner came to me with a terrible story: She had been walking through the market place in Brixton alone when she was approached by a stranger. This stranger told her that she had an astral worm consuming her insides and doing terrible things to her. After a while, this young woman became panic-stricken.

The stranger told her that he had a cure for this terrible worm. All she had to do was to buy this jar of bath salts and the worm would disintegrate. But the bath salts were expensive because they were so rare. It would cost £600 per jar. If she didn't have £600, then she must save her life by stealing and selling her mother's jewellery. In fact, the young woman sold everything she had and handed over the money. Very distressed, she brought her purchase to show me and I found they were *my* bath salts that the trickster had paid £3.00 for.

There are confidence tricksters about. I don't like it. Members of the Craft don't like it. These con-men give us all a bad name. That jar of bath salts cost me £2 to produce, not £600. This stranger was sent back to his own country by Her Majesty's police force - good! If anyone tries this stunt on you, the nearest policeman might be very interested in such a con-man. Please do not surrender any money. Walk away without opening your wallet or cheque book.

Some of you who live in London and use the Underground may have emerged to find a man or woman handing out leaflets. The leaflets advertise 'Brother Frankenstein' or 'Sister Starlight' or some such name. The leaflet says that Sister Starlight can help you, whatever your problem. The problem might be a wayward lover, shortage of cash, alcoholism of a member of your family. Appointments

to see Sister S. are not always necessary, please come along.

You may go along and at the first, or more usually the second, meeting, Sister Starlight will put the bite on you. She will tell you that you have a terrible curse on you and that it will cost £1,500 to take it off. And, of course, you must be silent about such a magical work. (Obviously if you tell anyone, they might take you to see a psychiatrist!)

The price doesn't stay at £1,500, it goes up and up from there. Sister Starlight and her kind will take every cent you have. And if you have a stack of notes put by for your life savings, then Sister Starlight will tell you that this money must be ritually cleaned in her temple, just bring it along and you can have it back next week. But when you go to get your money back, Sister Starlight has moved, leaving no forwarding address.

This is NOTHING to do with Witchcraft. It is a confidence trick, pure and simple. It targets the vulnerable, the love-sick, the lonely, and the elderly. It also targets people who are unlikely to go to the police and admit they've been foolish. We have no idea how much money Sister Starlight and her aliases have made. I have had several of her victims come to me for help. I don't like this con-game and neither does anyone else in the occult world. If you find someone operating this game and trying to take money off you, go and talk to the police. The police can do nothing without information. They need *your* information.

And, incidentally, if you want to cleanse money, you can put it in a pile and place on top of it a pentagram or a cross, or a star of David or whatever your religious symbol is. You tell the pentagram, or whatever, "Please cleanse this money in the name of (your favourite God or Goddess)" and you leave it overnight. In the morning, you thank your God or Goddess and you now have cleansed money. Simple? Yes. And I hope it hasn't cost you a penny!

CRAFT AND PRIORITIES

The modern Witch is required to know *The Book of Shadows* - it should be committed to memory. He or she should be efficient in astrology and practised in herbal lore. They should know seasonal and weather lore, numerology, palmistry, divination etc. They must be able to make lucky charms, amulets and talismans. They must know their way around Art Magic and Ritual Magic. Above all, they must be able to inspire confidence in those who ask for help. And they must be able to use psychic powers for healing.

All of which is a tall order for one person. In a modern coven it is usual for one or two members to handle the astrology, someone else will deal with herbs whilst another Witch instructs on the different facets of the Craft. The Witch is taught that in the old days, the Wise Ones were versed in all the requirements of the Craft and had committed most if not all of their knowledge to memory.

Because of today's demands, Witches have less time for their practices than their predecessors. It is certainly permissible to divide responsibility and achievement. The Astrologer chooses the right time to perform certain ceremonies. He will also select the best moments for constructing charms and talismans. He will decide the right hour for a new member's initiation ceremony so that they exert the correct influences on other coven members.

He may hold classes to instruct others on how astrology applies to ritual magic. Possibly he will delay or bring forward a meeting night because of the planetary influences on the day originally selected. He rarely works as a professional astrologer for the public. One coven operated without a 'Resident Astrologer' for some time, availing itself of an astrologer outside the movement but sympathetic to the cause.

The Herbalist or plant expert with his specialised knowledge is of equal importance and works closely with the Astrologer. All

those of my acquaintance have been dedicated followers of nature for years and their expertise in their beloved work is a wonderful understanding to share with them. They give generously of their knowledge, often inheriting their gift from father or mother, rarely referring to the printed word. In this department of the Craft too, decoctions, philtres and potions are available in the event of a coven having no practitioner. There are flourishing businesses in their field for anyone who wants to experiment with herbs.

Progress and spiritual development are in the hands of the High Priestess and the High Priest. Using exercises, yoga and their own special methods, they can do much to improve the individual's psychic capabilities. They will also use invocation and herbal mixtures to induce trances if they feel that their pupil will benefit.

I have known Witches to look at you on the first meeting and reel off details about you they could not have known from any other source of information. They will probably tell you something of your 'psychic picture' and, perhaps, a bit about your future. No Witch in her right mind will claim to predict all your future with complete accuracy, but many people approach them for just such a purpose; thus Witches study the different methods of divination.

Apart from astrology and palmistry, the principal methods of divination and character assessment, Witches study the more obscure methods which have been in use over the years. The tarot is also used for divination and in the opinion of some people quite wrongly. Other methods include cartomancy, the use of playing cards, and graphology for character assessment, and suitability of career.

Dream interpretation, dice, tea cups, all these have been used. Precious stones may be cast and their resultant position analysed. Flowers have also been used. The resurgence of interest in the I Ching and also the ancient runes have resulted in requests for readings by these methods.

Of course the Witch is not required to have all this knowledge ready for immediate use. Some of those interested in the spheres of low divination delight in using the more obscure methods, just for the sake of appearance. Some of the official interpretations of omens are staggering, and some of the methods seem just plain childish, but all respond to the rule of thumb: "If it works, use it."

After all, if you were told by a Witch that she used ceremancy, metapomancy and lampadomancy, you would have to be impressed and the Witch's reputation would grow. You don't know what these mean?

1. Ceremancy - interpretation of the shape of melting wax dropped on the floor.
2. Metapomancy - interpretation of the lines on your forehead.
3. Lampadomancy - divination from the flame of a lamp.

DEATH TAKES A BROOMSTICK

Witchcraft is a very ancient religion, indeed it was the original religion of this country, long before the Christian church came along to convert us. Its people believed in an afterlife. They took the line that death was no more than a gateway. The Dark Goddess would receive them and take them under her cloak to sleep for a while and then they would wake up in 'paradise'.

What was Paradise like for the Witch? Well, these islands were very cold in winter so Paradise was warm. Most people had little fuel so paradise was 'The Summer Land'. Hunger was a common complaint so the Witch's paradise had plenty of food and feasting. Most people had lost friends or relatives that they loved and those

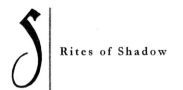

friends would be waiting to greet them. This heaven may not sound too much like a Holy City of gold and jewels but it echoed the real desires of early pagan people. They would wake in an apple orchard where it was always summer. There would be the sound of tinkling bells in the air. They would meet their friends and feast with their God and Goddess. There they would play until the time when the Goddess decided to send them back to earth for another incarnation.

There is even a delightful Witchcraft legend which states that the Witch will waken in the orchard and the first thing she will see are her beloved pets who have gone before her. The Goddess allows all her creatures into heaven. To many of us, this sounds a very pleasant afterlife indeed!

In Craft tradition, the Witch should leave her magical equipment to another Witch for proper disposal. Daggers, wands, cups and so on must not fall into unauthorised hands. In practice, the Witch makes a will like anyone else. I have talked to several solicitors about this and both have advised against using the word 'Witchcraft' in a will. They advised the use of the words, 'theatrical props, costumes and scripts' instead. It is alright to leave theatrical stuff to a friend but you must not leave Witchcraft items in case someone questions your sanity!

The Witch may die at home, or in hospital. Christian relatives seem to emerge from the woodwork at this point and suggest that the deceased should be buried in their graveyard, whether the Witch would approve or not. It is not unusual for a meeting of the coven to gather shortly afterwards and hold a farewell service in memory of their departed friend. If there is a singer among the coven members, a mourning song may be sung at the meeting and so an example is included in this book. There would also be a brief speech from the High Priestess reminding coven members that we will all meet again.

If possible, the silver ring of the Witch remains on her finger at death, to remind her that she is a child of the Goddess. A few leaves from an apple tree may also be put into the coffin. Should the Witch be cremated, the High Priestess might scatter the ashes in some pagan holy spot. I have had to organise this sort of thing on a number of occasions over the years. Although some Christian people have been a little uncomfortable about it, a Craft coven can do a sensible job when one of its members goes off to the Summerland.

THE WITCH'S CURSE

Witches seldom curse, although tradition suggests otherwise. There is an old saying, "Curses, like rooks, come home to roost." An ill-conceived curse is more likely to affect the Witch whilst the victim gets off scot-free.

There are a few times when the Witch has a right to protest. I would sympathise with a Witch being burnt at the stake and cursing her murderers. I would sympathise with a curse on a politician who tried to bring back the old Witchcraft Act. I wouldn't waste time cursing someone who stole my parking space because it would be misuse of power.

Recently there was a just curse put out. Witches held a piece of land where meetings could take place. Also on that land was a graveyard for cats, a gravestone, a small altar, a 'magic' circle and a place for hiding Witchcraft equipment. Thieves moved in. They stole a Witch's altar, the gravestone and they took all the equipment. The police were not interested. We were prepared to put up a reward but the local paper would not take the advertisement because they felt that people might get upset. (Presumably they did not think the Witches were upset at desecration!)

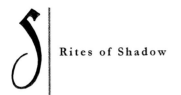

None of us had stolen anything from the church, nor had we defaced gravestones or anything. I assume that the thieves were of Christian background, although one might doubt their religious beliefs, or whether they had any. I am totally mystified by the theft of a cat's gravestone which would have no value to anyone else. All we wanted was to be left alone to practise our religion. Deprived of normal justice, a curse was put out on the thieves by the High Priestess. I reprint that curse here, although it does not occur in *The Book of Shadows.*

Lift, O lift the scales of Fate,
Be the sword perceived too late,
By the curse from distant past
Be the shadow free at last.
In the hourglass falls the sand,
Brunnisende, raise thy hand,
Weave the curse on those profane,
Shadow, weave a silken skein,
Answer thou the Witches lore,
Shadow, take them evermore,

Gather, Darkness.

There is a moral to this story. We try to be nice people. We try to get on with our religious practices quietly, offending no one. We don't approve of desecration.

Don't push a Witch too far.

SUMMARY

Witchcraft is fundamentally a religion, and it is the prime concern of all to promote the study of its history, its comparison with other pagan religions and the established church, and its practice.

The Craft was in evidence long before the established Church in this country. Some say that it can be traced back to the dawn of time. Witchcraft is a religion of fertility and sympathetic magic plus a constant ambition to develop spiritually, physically and mentally at all times. Into the basic worship of the Moon Goddess and the Horned God has come a form of ritual celebration, mixed with Qabalistic magic and watered down pseudo-Egyptian occultism. Certainly Witchcraft today bears no resemblance to the highly-imaginative medieval church publications. All a Witch wants is to be left alone to enjoy the fruits of a belief and the satisfaction that religious worship can give.

After having studied the history of Witchcraft from both without and within a coven, it is a constant source of amazement to me that it can still flourish. So many anti-Witch writings from so many biased and learned people have smeared the movement with malignancy and ignorance that in ordinary circumstances would occasion slander and libel actions. Much of the history of the Craft is concerned with the number of people who died for it. Much more of the history would out-do any book on torture today.

Not surprisingly, Craft members opt for secrecy for much of their work. Unfortunately this secrecy allows the press and the public to dream up any fiction they like, 'nameless rites', indescribable horrors and all the rest. It may indeed be the dawn of a New Age but I see a number of people piling up bits of wood in the market place.

I am convinced that there is much danger within the 'secrecy' of the Craft. Many practitioners are sincere people who lead normal

and blameless lives. They stay within the civil law. They do not work their spells naked on a blasted heath. They do not scourge each other and they do not go in for orgies. Far from doing animal mutilation or molesting children, the majority of Witches do a tremendous amount of charity work. They are not ignorant people. I had one very dear Witch friend who was well ahead with her work on ecology before most people had ever heard of the word. She knew more about global warming than most people today. These people are not old-fashioned eccentrics. They are not just streets ahead of the public, they are light years ahead.

Witches are blamed by press and television for terrible things. They are blamed for pushing drugs, seducing the young, corrupting everything, disturbing marriages, blighting fields, animal mutilation, child molestation, making crop circles, causing death and so on. They are even blamed for ritual murders.

It is time that the 'secrecy' was dropped. It is time that the spells and *The Book of Shadows* be put under microscopes and examined. Perhaps this book will further a better understanding all around.

THE
BOOK
OF
SHADOWS

I acknowledge the help of the Witch friend Kemmoc in dealing with this manuscript.

I owe much to other people within the Craft but their names cannot be mentioned for many reasons.

I also acknowledge the hindrance of a Coven whose Death Curse I have braved in publishing these writings. Their curses didn't help me at all.

THE BOOK OF SHADOWS

Keep *The Book of Shadows* in your own handwriting.

Give to your fellow workers the spells that they need, but your book shall not leave your hands. Hide your book within a secret place and learn from it as much as you can. One day it may become necessary to destroy your *Book of Shadows*, but when the time of necessity has passed, you shall re-write your book with care and accuracy.

The history of the Craft is a history of persecution and misunderstanding. The possession of a *Book of Spells* meant torture and death. The Burning Time has ended long ago, but what has happened once may happen again in time. Yet if a time of persecution shall come once more, see that you do not betray the names of your associates. Remember that in the Burning Time, others suffered torture rather than betray their Craft. In those days, drugs were given them to ease their pain and death came before the fire. And if this history repeats itself, your associates will come to your aid if you betray them not.

Seek not to attract attention, for our traditional safety lies in secrecy and though we made magic, we used mostly common household articles for our Craft. Therefore boast not of Witch power. Threaten no man with illness of evil happenings. Seek not to impress the credulous with strange knowledge but rather hide your secrets from the eyes of those who would not understand. Speak not of the Craft to outsiders and keep the knowledge secret, even in this day.

If you are in trouble, then remember all those who have gone before the God and the Goddess and remember their endurance. Confess to nothing if it can be avoided. Remember that if you are questioned by anyone, it is better to speak total foolishness and lie, rather than permit the secret knowledge to be betrayed. It is better to be laughed at rather than to suffer another Burning Time when many people who were not of the Craft were killed by fear and greed.

The Faith of the Craft

We worship the God that men fear, the Horned God of ancient days. We worship the Goddess, the Lady of older times. And the God is the Sun God of life and strength, but he is also the Dark Lord of peace and understanding. And the Goddess is the Maid of Joy and Hope. She is the Mother of love and protection. Yet she is also the Dark Lady of peace, wisdom and magic. Yet beyond these two, our Lord and our Lady, is the One we do not know, that which we cannot name or limit, for the One is limitless.

We work our Craft in the names of the Lord and the Lady. Every spell that we have, every magic that we work and every act in life is done before these two. We carry a part of each within ourselves, but the Lord and the Lady are above us. Through our Craft do we serve the Lord and the Lady and do what best we can to serve our fellow men without the Craft.

On Obedience

For as long as you shall remain within the Coven circle, you shall be obedient to the High Priestess. You shall listen to her words at all times for she is the representative of our Mother, the Goddess, and her words are those which rule us.

You shall not fail to obey the command of the High Priestess during any ritual, no matter what the command shall be. The High Priestess is there to aid you and other children of the Goddess, therefore you shall act upon her words, even if you do not immediately see the reason for her instructions.

For between you and the High Priestess there shall be OBEDIENCE.

The Five Essentials

The most important is INTENTION. You must know what you are there to do and you must know that you will succeed.

You must PREPARE everything properly beforehand and check that it is rightly prepared and that everything lies in readiness.

The Circle must be cast correctly and then purified.

You yourself must be purified, both bodily and spiritually. [A ritual bath is a new idea for Craft members, but it is a very good idea.] And before you start your ceremony, you must cast from you hate and malice and any evil that is in you. If this is not done, the ceremony may work very differently to your stated intentions.

You must have properly consecrated tools.

The Eight-Fold Ways

1. Concentration, activated by the firm knowledge that you can and will succeed. Form a clear picture in your mind of all your requirements accomplished.
2. Trance states - these include the use of clairvoyance and astral travel.
3. Herbal knowledge, incense and wine.
4. Performing rites with a purpose.
5. The use of the Dance.
6. The use of chants and spells.
7. Body control.
8. Total involvement in worship.

The Greater & Lesser Sabbats

The Sabbats are May Eve - 30th April, sometimes called Roodmass, Roodday and Walpurgis night. The last of these names is, strictly speaking, a German name and was not used in this country.

There is a Sabbat on November Eve which is known to the Craft as Souwain, or Samhain, and to the Christians as Hallowe'en.

Between these come Candlemas (2nd of February) and the Gales of August, (31st) also known as Lammas.

The solstices and equinoxes are also celebrated by Craft members, the first day of spring, Midsummer day, the beginning of the autumn and the shortest day of the year. Actually the dates of these days vary and are best looked up in your current diary.

The Esbat was the Small Assembly which took place at the local meeting point, primarily for business reports, cures, local magic and 'any other business', whereas the Sabbat was usually religious, although one exception might be made for this rule. The exception was May Eve, for this was regarded as a time of feasting and merriment.

The primitive manner of life was a constant battle for survival against an environment which was seldom over-generous. Food was the first necessity of life and, as man learned to hunt, the woman become protector, healer, mother and nurse. In a fortified village settlement, it was the woman's responsibility to acquire and pass on the knowledge of healing herbs etc. Hence she became the prototype of the Mother Goddess who symbolises rest, pleasure, contentment, love and life.

Festivals

In some of the festivals in the olden days, when the meetings were held a little distance from the village, it was a custom to bring at least one broomstick to the meeting. The purpose behind the custom was the use of the broomstick as something to jump over, the higher you jumped, the higher the corn would grow and so the better the harvest. However, in the general 'horseplay' and merry-making, the broomstick was ridden and sometimes even used as a dancing partner. This gave rise to the legend that all Witches rode broomsticks.

It was also customary to have seasonal branches and flowers at a Craft meeting, i.e. blossoms in May time, green branches in August, autumn leaves at Hallowe'en and evergreens at Candlemas.

One must remember that the traditions of the Craft date back to the time before street lighting and cars. A Craft meeting place that was half a mile away from the village was considered far away from anywhere. It was safe to light a fire in such a place, and one could make a noise without being noticed. No policemen would appear to see what was going on. In a civilisation that was based on sunrise and sunset, it was perfectly safe to meet at midnight, so long as you were home at sunrise. It was a matter of safety.

Sweet smelling herbs and woods were always thrown into the fire before and after the dancing. Today it is seldom possible to dance in the open air and very often the space available in modern houses and flats makes dancing impossible anyway.

Miscellaneous Notes

It is a common belief that Witches cast love spells, and there are all sorts of recipes purporting to cause love to grow between two people. In strict Craft law, it is not considered legal to force an un-willing woman or man into love by use of a spell, although this ruling might be waived to force a hesitant lover to make a proposal of marriage etc. It is not considered legal to deprive an-other of his or her will.

Many Witches would argue against mending a marriage if it appeared that both parties would be happier elsewhere. Craft mem-bers were supposed to know the plants with aphrodisiac powers. They were also supposed to know the plants which could cause abortions and, whilst there are different ethics on this last problem, it was reckoned a useful accomplishment in war-torn lands where rape was a common occurrence.

The Esbat is the Small Assembly of the local coven. It is some-times held at the full of the moon and sometimes at the new moon.

A man is usually initiated into the Craft by a woman and a woman is usually initiated by a man. Exceptions to this rule crop up from time to time where a solitary man or woman, perhaps not in contact with any other member of the Craft, instructs one of the same sex in useful spells.

Occasionally at a Craft meeting a man is asked to represent the God and a woman is asked to represent the Goddess. The key word is 'represent' - it does not mean imitate!

The original concern of the Craft was the fertility of the land; the ever present problem of food and its storage. Today this has taken 'second place' for many Craft members who are city dwellers with cars to go to the nearest supermarket and fridge-freezers in their kitchens. They can leave the scientists and agriculture experts to deal with problems of food and storage. However, it might prove unwise to forget this concern lest we find that genetically engineered food brings mankind a whole new load of problems.

Fertility problems were associated with a High Priestess of the Craft. In days gone by, she had to be a skilled lady, able to say what the weather would do. She had to know everything about which seeds to sow and when to harvest them. She was probably the oldest woman present at a village gathering. The custom has given rise to the idea that Witches were all old women on broomsticks, but the oldest woman was always supposed to be wise in her ways. Ever remember that it is the duty of those in the Craft to help those who ask for aid, if help can be given.

The traditional colour of the Witches is green, the colour of growth, considered by many outside the Craft to be an unlucky colour.

Remember that when we are within the circle of the Craft, what happens within the circle is the concern of both worlds.

Keep your clothing for the Craft in a secret place, and wear it not for any lesser worship. Let it be clean and well prepared for sudden usage. And before you put on your clothing, remember that you put from you your ordinary self. And you put on the robe of the Craft, asking the Lord and the Lady that you be clean of heart for you to do your work.

Although it is in no way essential, some Craft women wear a ceremonial bracelet. This is always made of silver and usually about 2" broad. It is often engraved with a Craft name in one of the secret scripts, together with the proper signs of rank or the sign of the pentagram. Mostly the engraving is done inside the bracelet.

Scourging

Though this is not a part of our native Craft, there are those of the Craft who feel that it must be done, the men receiving it first and the women afterwards. There are various ideas about the number of strokes to be given, but the usual number is forty strokes.

Scourging is in direct conflict with the CHARGE which states that one does not harm one's own body, or any other body; the body is a gift from the Lord and the Lady.

To Get The Sight

Every child is born with the magical sight, yet some children reject that sight for themselves. Some children are even punished for seeing into the spiritual world. Discouraging a child from having magical sight is regarded as a crime, but occasionally a Craft member will counsel a child not to speak of all it sees, lest the child bring trouble on its own head.

The adult who desires to increase magical sight often does it with the help of meditation and incense. Each one endeavours to relax and allow the atmosphere to build up, using music and incense to stimulate the senses. There are many incenses that can be bought today, and many more incense recipes that appear in obscure books of learning. Yet the Witch must ever remember that vision is not reality and the two must not be confused.

The Meeting Dance

The dance is led by a man or a maiden, depending on the ceremony, but whichever shall lead, the other shall follow alternately, man and woman. It is reckoned that a dance which follows the path of the sun is the proper way and the dance that runs against the sun is a dance of evil.

The Commemorative Dance

If a dance is done to commemorate an event in the past, it must be done not simply as a representation of the event, but to make all those present remember everything that was involved. You must dance your magical purpose, and you must dance it with feeling and desire. Mime dances are an ancient tradition, lost in the dawn of time. Those that have come down to us in English folklore are sometimes confused and require careful research. It is better not to mime some forgotten battle and misinterpret a dance, for the mis-interpretation will bring about unhappy results. Rather mime some new dance than follow an ancient formula that means something very different to your desire.

The Tools of the Craft

From the dawn of time, the Craft members have made their own tools, and it is right to do so. It is not always possible to make your own equipment, but even if you buy your tools, you alone must consecrate them.

There is only one exception to this rule: You never buy your own silver cup. This is always a present from another practitioner of the Craft.

The Altar

Traditionally this is a small table, such as is found in any household. If it is possible, your altar should be set apart and not used for any other thing. Yet if this is not possible, then when in use you cover the table with a clean white cloth and put only a vase of flowers upon it. Do not use this table for anything else save for your craft workings.

The Secret Place

Of old, those who followed the Craft were taught to hide the tools of their work within some secret place. If possible, this place should be near to the place where you sleep. Be certain that the tools of your craft are locked away, and let no one touch them. Your tools are not loaned to others within the Craft. They are not given away, save for the cup which must be given with love.

You shall not use tools that are bought in the market place but are not new. You know not who has used such tools or what their aims might be. Nor shall you inherit tools from any unknown source. But, having your own tools, you shall keep them in a secret place and ask protection that your secret is not discovered lest it bring trouble upon you. [Remember too that theft is common in this age. You may devise a secret place, but a thief with time on his hands will tear your place apart to find hidden valuables. Nor will he treat your religious items with any respect. Those items will probably turn up in a car boot sale! Having a secret place is a wonderful thing, but if it remains secret, then you are fortunate indeed.]

Incense

For good results, it is best to buy a proper incense. Traditionally we make our own incense from sweet smelling herbs such as rosemary, thyme and basil. A chafing dish of hot coal is used for burning the herbs. Use not a censer for, though these can be bought, they are not a part of the Craft and may lead to the accusation that you have robbed a church.

Many Craft practitioners today prefer to use one of the small burners and scented oils. This is a practical way of scenting a small room and perfectly sensible for someone living in a small flat where the smoke of incense would set off fire alarms etc.

The Cup & The Platter

During the time of the persecution, no special magical equipment was marked or set aside in any way, lest a search reveal it to the authorities. The cup used in a Craft ceremony was simply the best cup in the household, and the platter (or plate) likewise. These were not made of silver or gold lest we were accused of withholding taxes or thieving from the Church. Nor were the cup and platter

marked in any way outwardly, but rather consecrated with the sign of the Pentagram drawn on them in charged water. In that way they were sacred to the Lord and the Lady from that time forth.

Today the cup and the platter are made of the best materials that you can afford. They remain hidden away in a secret place and they are used only in the cakes and wine ceremony.

The Athamé

Athamé is the word for a black handled knife used in Craft working. Of old, a knife was the most useful tool in a household. The knife was made of iron with a hilt which should be fashioned out of box wood. It was not marked with any magical sign. Today's knives are often marked with secret writings and signs of power.

The White-Handled Knife

This was essential to some Craft members. It is likewise made of iron and put away until it is needed.

The Sword

Traditionally you had no sword unless you had actually fought in a war, for the presence of a sword in a household where Witchcraft was suspected would have damned every member of the household. Nor are names of power engraved upon the sword, for this would have been held as evidence of trafficking with the Devil. In fact the sword is simply an extension of the knife and not strictly necessary for practising Craft members. Remember that a sword engraved with magical signs cannot easily be concealed, and a consecrated sword must not be drawn without the greatest care.

The Wand

This you shall cut yourself using the consecrated athamé. You shall go out before dawn on Midsummer day and choose a proper tree to cut it from as the sun arises. Or you shall cut your wand when the stars are most propitious to you. And, having cut the wand, you shall take it to your dwelling in a bag and let no one see it or handle it, before or after it is consecrated.

The Scourge

This is not a part of our tradition. If you desire to make such a thing, you shall cut a stick and bind it with cords. Let there be eight cords and each cord shall be knotted five times.

The Pentagram

The Pentagram is the sign of the Craft, the interlocking five pointed star of hope for the future. This is sometimes engraved on a flat piece of copper which may be used for the Cakes and Wine ceremony. It used to be drawn on to a plate in ink and washed off immediately after use, as the possession of such an object would be deemed proof of black magic. Today the sign of the pentagram can be engraved on a sheet of copper or even a silver plate.

To Mark Out a Circle

In order to mark out a new circle, measure out a cord to be 4' 6" (137 cm) long with a loop at one end. Place your athamé point downwards in the centre of the ground or room and slip the loop over the end of the handle of the knife. Using the length of cord as a radius, draw out the circle in the ground with another knife or pointed stick, and then re-trace the circle using the athamé. Always renew the circle as you use it, but you can have it permanently marked out on private ground so that it is always in the same place.

Remember that the circle being properly made and consecrated must prevent the magical power from being dissipated instead of being applied. The circle holds the power IN.

The circle is also a protection against disturbing or mischievous forces. Whilst it is being prepared, a 'gateway' is left in the circle for members to enter. Once the circle is completed, no one may enter or leave before the ceremony has ended.

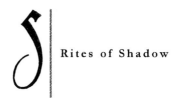

Craft Rituals

Always remember that Craft workings are best done collectively by a number of associates who feel the same emotions. The earliest Craft rituals were more concerned with food than anything else, for food meant survival. Our ancestors sought the aid of the Lord and the Lady within the circle with that end in mind. They desired most sincerely to multiply plants, animals and children. Ritual bridges the gulf between real life and total worship. The original aims have been passed on to today's Craft members, yet the Craft has broadened and become a study and the rituals must be regarded in the light of the changing days and the New Age.

It is essential to maintain order and discipline at a meeting if worship is to be done or anything is to be accomplished. Harken and heed the words of the Priestess or Priest who presides over the meeting, lest it degenerate into disorder.

The Lord and the Lady alone see the true colours of each heart and know who merits punishment and who shall have praise. Only they have the right to punish the faults of a coven member. Yet if a member of the Craft has caused trouble within the Circle, it is better to bid that person to be gone rather than to cause evil unto him. Justice and Mercy are not in your hands. You are not the God or the Goddess, therefore seek not to punish, but leave such things unto those who we worship.

Remember that we do not seek to be the enemy of any man. We strive to be the friend of that which IS eternally.

We seek no quarrel with any man, but rather we seek that quarrels may be swiftly reconciled. If anyone should devise evil against us, then we seek to escape without harm and without the need of hurting those who plot against us.

May we seek to attain only those things which are good and true, and considered to be the blessings of the Ancient Ones, LOVE, FREEDOM, HAPPINESS AND PEACE.

On Safe Working in the Circle

For your own safety, consider well the following rules that are written by one with great experience:

1. If you work in the open air, then inspect the site beforehand and ascertain that none can oversee you. This is a twenty-four hour civilisation and a lot of people have cars. Finding an isolated spot can be difficult. It is a good idea to have a fall-back plan. If an outsider is watching, then they will spread a lying report of that which you do and this will cause trouble to practitioners of the Craft.

2. If you work within a house, then make sure that it is empty of other humans. Remember, when you have finished your ritual, you must close down the power lest others take fright at the nearness of the unseen world.

3. Design your robes for the Craft as simply as possible. Remember you may be dancing in those robes so they must not be over-long to trip you up. Sleeves should be fairly tight so that nothing is knocked off the altar. Cloaks are made to conceal the identity of the wearer. Masks, if worn, may impede your vision. The tall hat of the fairy-tale Witch will certainly fly off in a wind unless firmly tied to your head and they also come off if you're dancing!

4. Before commencing any ceremony, make certain that everything you need is within the Witch's circle. Apart from the basic initiation when someone is sent out to fetch a candidate, no one should ever leave a circle in the middle of a ritual. It is bad technique and it can be very dangerous.

5. Fire is not the only element that can cause trouble. Any of the elements can get out of control in a magical working. However, fire can be a spectacular trouble-maker if there is an angry elemental behind it. All candles should be fixed firmly in place before you start your ceremony. Bonfires out of doors must also be properly controlled. It is a good idea to wear fire resistant clothing. It is also a good idea to have a proper fire extin-

guisher within the circle. Do not take any chances with fire.

6. Bowls of charcoal and incense get very hot over a period of time, especially if the bowl is made of metal. Metal bowls can burn human skin and also char a wooden altar. You might try a layer of sand at the bottom of the bowl, or updating tradition here by consecrating an asbestos plate and placing it beneath the incense bowl. Do not touch the bowl once the incense is alight. Some covens use a censer. This is not a traditional tool of the Craft, but occasionally you come across a ritual which requires someone to pace around the Circle a number of times, censing it as they walk. Obviously carrying a burning hot plate of charcoal and incense is not practical, and so a censer is used for this sort of proceedings. Censers are, however, quite tricky to work. The chains tend to become tangled up and they can spill burning charcoal all over the floor. The best rule is to insist that everyone stands still whilst the censer is being used. Only one person moves and he, or she, walks three times around the Circle, or nine times or however many times you feel necessary. When you finish with the censer, hang it up somewhere out of the way. Like the plate, it gets too hot to leave it standing on an altar. The chains of a censer will get tangled into unbelievable knots. Use a censer properly or don't use a censer at all. You have a possible update. You could use a perfume oil burner instead of the more traditional bowl full of charcoal and incense. It is less overpowering in a small room and you will not have to grope your way through smoke. It you are working in a small room, please remember that a very little incense can go a long way. A salt-spoon of incense may be adequate. Start with very little incense and experiment from there. You don't want to make your house uninhabitable.

7. Cleaning tools and temple silver, or copper, is a job which must be done by a member of the coven, NOT by an outsider. Do not clean a metal cup with a cyanide based silver polish if you, or anyone else, intend to drink from that cup. Wash it and pol-

ish it with elbow grease instead! Silver varnish is a useful invention and very handy when it comes to silver plate. Use it.

8. Make arrangements that, in case of accident, another member has access to your tools. All sorts of troubles crop up when the instruments of the Craft turn up at a boot sale or on a stall in Portobello Road. The general public regard these items as curios. They handle them without knowing what they are. They might buy a pretty little dagger and take it home not realising that there is a fire elemental attached. A vicar might buy your censer. If you cannot dispose of your own tools and robes, someone else of your tradition must be able to do so for you.

9. "Please" and "Thank you" are words of power. You cannot command the Lord to do what you want. You cannot threaten the Goddess with anything. If you try to bully, browbeat, command, threaten or bribe the unseen world, you will only succeed in convincing the unseen world that you are incredibly stupid. Ask for something by all means but remember that "No" is an answer, even if it isn't the answer that you wanted. And thank the Powers who have aided you when you finish.

10. If you are planning to work an unfamiliar ceremony, take the time to rehearse beforehand. Don't 'rush' through it because someone wants to take an early train home.

11. A coven member in bad health should not dance or exert themselves because you do NOT want a corpse on your hands, nor do you want anyone passing out during a ceremony.

12. Allow a certain amount of time for the power to 'die down' at the end of a ceremony. It is NOT good technique to leave a place magically 'alive' - it frightens the skin off ordinary human beings and it can affect animals as well. Close down your ceremony properly when the working is finished, and may the Lord and the Lady bless you.

Success

You shall remember that the success or failure of any operation lies not in the tools that you have, but rather in the mental attitude

of the operator. If you are not keyed up to high pitch when you work your ceremony, you will not attain success.

The Purpose

You shall state the purpose of your ceremony clearly, so that all present may know the object in view and desire that object most dearly. The simple tools described will aid you and, properly consecrated, the tools are an extension of yourself. Those tools are not regarded as outside objects or 'curiosities'. They are a part of you and all your power and they should be near you always.

The athamé should lie beneath your pillow for months. Today's Witch often carries the athamé in a handbag or briefcase. No one handles your tools save you yourself, the exception to this rule being a pair of Craft members living and working together. These may use the same tools.

The Pattern

The majority of Craft workings conform to a pattern. When all are met and the circle is prepared, the High Priestess stands before the altar, raises her hands in a gesture of invocation and says *"Let the ceremony begin"*.

1.   There is always a prayer for protection.

2.   There is a 'statement of purpose'

3.   Any special magical working follows and then comes the seasonal celebration.

4.   Initiations are usually followed by cakes and wine.

5.   There is often a pause for 'any other business' - healing a sick animal, a prayer for a sick child to get over chickenpox quickly; it is usually something that a Craft Member would like to help with, but not something big enough to be the main purpose of the ritual.

6.   Announcements are made, maybe even the date, time and place of the next meeting are read out. The last is a modern tradition, not an ancient one. In earlier days the date, time and place of

the next meeting would have been kept secret until just before the meeting took place.

7.   Finally a closing prayer is read by the High Priestess, who then says, *"Before the God and the Goddess, the meeting is ended"*.

8.   Though the formal Craft meeting is ended, many of the workings are followed by a feast or party of some kind, and possibly even dancing.

Invocation & Consecration of the Circle

First draw the Circle with the athamé or sword. Consecrate salt and water as follows:

"Be this salt dedicated to the Lord and the Lady to keep us from evil and to protect us in this time.
Be this water dedicated to the Lord and the Lady to keep us from peril and to purify this place."

Mix the salt and the water together and sprinkle sunwise around the circle.

"May we cast from us all evil and darkness, viciousness and malice. May we become that which we were before the Lord and the Lady, seeking ill to no one. May we be clean within and without that we are acceptable before Them."

Invocations should start in the East and proceed SUNWISE, ending at the North for this reason. The North is the place of power which flows from North to South. The operator, being in the East, works up to the right. Having reached the North point, the Circle must still be closed so that there is no gap in it. The DEOSIL movement works up to the height. A WIDDERSHINS movement works downwards and is a movement of bad magic, cursing and so on.

The INVOCATION to form the circle is thus:
"O Mighty Powers of the East, I call upon you in this place and at this hour to keep safe our Circle and to guard and look upon these works."

Draw the invoking pentagram in the air. Now move to the South and repeat the invocation, only of course you invoke the Powers of the South. Draw the pentagram. Repeat this procedure to the West and the North and then turn to the East once more before you go to the Altar.

Candles should be in place at the North, South, East and West and you have learned to consecrate the fire upon the Altar. From this fire are lit the candles of the quarters at this stage.

An invocation is made to protect the Circle as follows:
Now the sacred Lady rises
New within the starlit sky,
Now, before the esbat meeting,
Guard us, Lady, by and by.
Wrap us in thy cloak of darkness,
Hide us in the mist of time,
Ere the spell is brewed and settled,
Hide us till the morning chime.
Guide us ere the dance commences,
Hide the cakes, conceal the wine,
Lead us from the age of darkness,
Sacred Queen and All Divine.
Guard us, Lord of Hunt and Forest,
By the power of fire and air,
As we come once more to worship,
Keep us, Witch Lord, in your care.
By the power of earth and water,
Now the circle spins and spins,
Come unto thy secret servants,
Guard us now the Rite begins.

After this invocation for protection, it is proper that the chafing dish of charcoal and incense shall be carried around the Circle. Such covens who insist on the use of the scourge will now use it. All now dance around the Altar using an invoking chant:

Thrice about the altar go,
Once for virgin pure as snow,
Once for full moon's soft sweet breath,
Once for dark moon, old as death,
Thrice about the altar spin,
That the Rite shall well begin.

Then shall be said the petition that everyone shall know the purpose of the ritual.

"*Witch Lord, Witch Lady, Sacred Pair that were before the dawn of time and shall be till the dusk, hear now the purpose of this ritual and witness it. For the ceremony is performed that ...* "
(Briefly and clearly state the purpose of the ritual.)

Now, to end the meeting, you shall do the same circling movement starting in the East and saying to the four quarters:

"*O Mighty Powers of the East, I thank you for guarding this Circle and for keeping us safe at this time. We bless thee in the name of the Lord and the Lady, in the name ZARACH and in the name ZARUNA.*"

You proceed to each quarter with your athamé or sword but you do NOT draw the pentagram.
Sometimes the requests to the powers of the quarters is made as follows:

"*Before the Lord and the Lady, I call upon the spirits of the East that they may come unto us to witness our sacred rites in the name of ZARACH and in the name of ZARUNA.*"

When the Circle is formed, the directions of North, South, East and West should be marked with candles. These are known as the candles of the quarters.

In some covens where the scourge is used, the High Priestess enters the Circle from the South West with her scourge in her left hand and her athamé in her right hand. She moves clockwise around the Circle to the East. She stops there, holding the instruments outstretched in the pentacle position. The rest of the coven enter for their ritual scourging and then the High Priestess draws the Circle and carries on as before.

The Closing of the Circle

High Priestess - (Except possibly Lammas when this may well be said by the High Priest):

"Companions, we have met together this night to celebrate the ... feast. Together we have worked for our purpose. The God and the Goddess have witnessed our workings and only they will measure all our purposes and all our hearts. Together we have invoked for power to accomplish our working, but it is not for us to command those whom we worship. Nor is it for us to bid them to be gone. We cannot dismiss them

"I ask instead of Zarach and Zaruna that they remain with us all our days, guiding our feet and lighting our paths. I ask that the Lord and the Lady are with us in our lives and in our deaths, our true parents, even as we are their children. Let the Circle be extinguished, but let us not forget our working of this night. Let the candles be put out, but let us not forget what we have learned. Let the rite be ended now in the knowledge that we shall meet once more.

"Before the Lord and the Lady, Zarach and Zaruna, God and Goddess, the meeting is ended."

Petition Poem

Lord of Hunt and Shining Queen,
Hear the word the witches speak,
Speak the words the witches know,
Now, within the midnight hour,
Grant us, Lord and Lady, power.
See upon the altar now
Cord and incense, wand and knife,
Cup and flame and water clear,
Cakes and wine for feasting hour,
Grant us, Lord and Lady, power.
Horned Hunter, Lady Moon,
See the spell become complete,
Take the wish behind the rite,
Bless it in this meeting hour,
Grant it, Lord and Lady, POWER

Calls

There were many chants and songs used in the gatherings and dances of ancient days. The meanings of many of these chants are forgotten, but we know they used cries of:

ARE - OW   ARE - OW   ARE - OW

and:

IR - AY, IR - AY, IRU - TAI

and also:

ALAB - AUOO

as well as:

PIRTU!

Other calls are:

OMORF - OR - EN

and, most powerful of all:

CROYKA

Chants

FAI, FAI, KUN OT KAL
FIR, FIR, KUN IT KAL
KLEET, FIR, KUN OT KAL
CROYKA, CROYKA, CROYKA.

SEMA, SEMA. SEMA,
META HARU TEI,
IBOX' ARMAGH TE
QUA OI ZIRE.

These are two ancient chants whose meanings are perhaps lost forever. A more modern Craft love chant is as follows:

I sew your shadow with my hair,
I bind your shadow unto me,
By day or night you shall remain
Before the Triple Goddess three,
I bind your shadow unto me,
Maiden, Mother, Hecate,
Dawn and noon and night-black sea,
Free thou art but bound to me
And thou art mine eternally.

A consecration of fire runs as follows:

Be to me the fire of moon,
Be to me the fire of night,
Be to me the fire of joy,
Turning darkness into light,
By the virgin waxing cold,
By the mother, full and bold,
By the hag queen, silent, old,
By the moon, the one in three,
Consecrated, BLESSED BE.

Craft tradition includes scarf magic - putting a spell on a scarf to keep the wearer safe, or even to strangle the wearer! This spell is used to send a scarf in search of a missing person:

Cloth twine and scarf creep,
Cloth search and cloth seek,
Scarf spelled and scarf blest,
Aid and guide me in my quest,
Scarf move and scarf search,
Scarf look and cloth lurch,
Scarf turn and twist and run,
Hoop and twine the spell begun,
Scarf of past and present bind,
Seek and search and search to find.

One of the Craft powers is that of working with illusions. Witches were supposed to cause storms at sea. Few people know that Craft members can make a phantom fleet of ships like that fleet which appeared on D-day. This is a chant which could well have been used for that operation:

Wind and water, moon and sea,
Make the phantom ships for me,

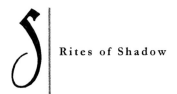

Moon and water, lose the sail,
Pass the fleet with sea swept gale,
Heave the ships in salt-drenched spray,
Moonlit mass have ships today,
Wind and moonlight, wind and dark,
Build a fleet of phantom barque,
Moon and water, wind and wave,
Carry phantom ships to save,
Wind and moonlight, storm and gale,
Creak the timbers, furl the sail,
Ghostly inmates serve the swell,
Man the ships that serve me well,
Moon and water, dark and free,
Guide my ships across the sea,
Sail the ships tonight for me.

Another love chant used by witches:

Dance the circle dance of dreaming,
Lonely by the crystal sea,
Spin the web of mist and moonlight,
Come, beloved, and follow me.

Chant the chant of souls entwining,
Round and through the sacred fire,
Drink from wells of mist and moonshine,
Lover, come to love's desire.

Dream the dreams of solemn passion
Through the star-encrusted night,
Weave the web of mist and moonfire,
Loved one, know all love's delight.

Hear the tides, the heaving waters
Sombre on the crystal sand,
Hear the chant of longing, waiting,
Come, fulfil at love's demand.

Seek and love my urgent body
Waiting nightly by the sea,
Tread the path of mist and moonlight,
Lover, come, beloved, to me.

And, as we promised in earlier in the book, here is a Craft mourning song for a coven member who has departed for the Summerland:

Yew tree, yew tree, understand our sorrow,
Tell the Queen of Darkness of a friendship still unending,
Dark tree, death tree, tree of dirge and mourning,
Whisper of our friendship to the winds that wail a-wending.

Yew tree, yew tree, know our timeless mourning,
Tell the Queen of Sorrow that our friendship lies aweeping,
Dark tree, dark tree, tree of death and anguish,
Whisper that our friend still lives, but say that she is
sleeping.

For earth of death is heaviness
And leaden lined in years,
And water for the yew tree's growth
Is water salt with tears,
And all the air that touches yew
Sings sorrow to the sky,
Whilst in the fire of yew tree wood
The stars grow pale and die.

Yew tree, yew tree, understand our sorrow
For a warm bright friendship that the fates saw fit to sever,
Dark tree, dark tree, we'll be re-united,
Tell the Queen of Heaven that our love endures forever.

Ancient Symbolism

The Pentagram is the symbol of the Craft and the star of our hope; though others also seek the star, this sign is our own.

The Cross in various patterns and variations is a very ancient symbol, but it symbolises Deity and man and the relationship between the two.

The Triangle, the geometrical sign of the three in one, is another ancient symbol. The triangle with apex pointed upwards symbolised the male and used with the point downwards, it is the female sign.

The poles, pillars etc. are the ancient symbols of the creative force of nature. Shafts, pylons, monolithic stones and so on are of phallic origin.

The Circle is the symbol of eternity, that without beginning or ending. It is sometimes known as the Ring.

The Celtic Cross or circle divided into four equal quarters is the division of the elements, the basic compass, the cycle of birth and death and so on.

Fruit, Plant & Tree Symbols

The oak is the tree of our power, as the willow tree is the one from which we weave bewitchments. The holly is the tree of the blood as the hazel tree is the bearer of the fruit of wisdom. The apple tree is the tree for lovers, but the evergreen trees, the elder and the yew were the trees of death.

But if you would bring an offering to the Goddess at Beltane, then bring to her blossoms and spring flowers. And if there is an offering at Lammas, then let it be of green branches and summer flowers. If there is an offering at Samhain, let it be ripe fruit and autumn leaves. And if you offer plant life at Candlemas, then the plants are the evergreen and such flowers as ye shall find in winter.

Words of the Mighty One

Keep your silence amidst the noise of the world, for there is still my peace within that silence.

Keep peace between yourself and other beings and listen to all men. Even the ignorant among mankind may perceive a truth you do not see. Surrender not your spirit to any other being, yet seek not battle but rather seek to avoid those people who trouble your spirit and spread trouble and vexation about them.

Seek not ambition too closely, for the most humble work must also be done, and properly done. This pleases the Lord and the Lady.

Those of the Craft are your brothers.

Speak not of the Craft to the outsider, for this world is plagued with misunderstandings. But remember that the world has also its virtues and ideals, and its people have their right to seek for Deity.

Strive to be gentle and understanding with your fellow men and be tolerant with their emotions, even if you do not understand them.

Regard the passing of the years without despair. Surrender the things of youth without sorrow, for age shall bring you deeper wisdom and greater understanding.

Study, then, the secret ways and cultivate the spiritual strength to shield you in unexpected misfortune.

Seek not to harm your own body, nor the body of any man or woman or child or animal, for all bodies are made of the substance of the earth and you shall not harm the Earth Mother. Therefore be gentle with yourself, for you are a child of the God and the Goddess.

Therefore care for your body, keeping it clean and healthy.

Disgrace not the Craft before your fellow men and bring not disrepute upon its followers.

Remember that you have walked upon this world before and shall walk it again in time. You may fill this world with broken dreams and sadness, and it may be that these shall stay with you for many lives. Yet this world is beautiful, though you may be blind to its beauty.

Therefore be careful. Seek and be happy.

Blesséd be

Consecration of a Sword or Athamé

If possible, partake of the cakes and the wine. The High Priest and the High Priestess say together:

"I conjure thee, O sword, that thou shalt serve me as a strength and a defence in every magical ceremony. Ye shall defend me against my enemies, both visible and invisible. In the Name of Zarach and in the Name of Zaruna."

[The High Priestess immerses the sword or athamé in charged water after which the High Priest passes the instrument through smoking incense. They both speak again.]

"I conjure thee again in the holy Name of Zarach and in the holy Name of Zaruna. O sword, serve me in adversity for my protection. So aid me now."

[The sword is laid with another consecrated sword upon the altar. The unconsecrated sword should be consecrated by an experienced Craft member who picks up the already consecrated weapon and presses it with the other. The High Priest and the High Priestess say together:]

"I conjure thee, O creature of steel, by the God and the Goddess whom we worship, by the waters and the winds, by the earth and by the fire, that in your virtue I shall attain my desire. Come when I call thee by this new name ... (name the instrument), *by the power of Zarach and Zaruna."*

If a sword and athamé have to be consecrated at the same time, then the High Priest shall press the sword to the sword and the High Priestess shall press the athamé to the new athamé. Both sword and athamé are then pressed to each other and then placed on the altar. When this ceremony is finished, the weapon or weapons are picked up by their new owner and must be pressed against the body for some time.

Ultimately the athamé becomes an extension of the Witch, so it must remain constantly with the owner for at least one month. No one else may touch your working tools as they are, strictly speaking, your own body and a part of yourself. You control your own tools all of the time, lest others work evil through you. A pair of Craft members, working together, can use the same tools, which become a mixture of both.

The Use of the Sword

Let it ever be remembered that a properly consecrated sword of the Craft must not lightly be unsheathed lest it bring quarrels and misfortune among those present. Use not the sword to impress others, for it is better to have no sword than to bring trouble amongst your associates or to unsheath it in an unjust quarrel.

Consecration of Other Tools

This includes the white-handled knife, the wand, the pentacle and the scourge if you use it. All these must be consecrated and blessed separately.

"Zarach and Zaruna, I call upon thee to bless this white-handled knife which I would consecrate and set aside. Let it obtain the necessary virtues for acts of beauty and love in the names of the Lord and the Lady."

The white-handled knife, or other instrument is then immersed in charged water, dried and held in the smoke of incense.

"Zarach and Zaruna, I call upon thee to bless this instrument which I have prepared in thine honour."

Repeat the water and incense smoke. Hold the instrument high in the air and say: *"Let blessing be."* Try to use the new tool as soon as possible.

Preparing the Cakes & Wine

The Cakes

These must be made of meal, salt, wine and honey. They should be shaped like a crescent moon. Put them to bake saying: *"Let the cakes be baked in the name of Zaruna, for now is the time of the ..... feast when the secret worshippers meet once more. Before the Goddess, we shall drain the cup. Before the Goddess we shall serve the secret rites. Before the Goddess we shall feast and rejoice. In the holy Name of Zaruna and in the holy Name of Zarach."*

The Wine
This should be home-made white wine, placed on the altar in a glass jug.
"Let the wine be made ready in the Name of Zarach and in the Name of Zaruna. Let it be placed upon the altar beneath the sign of the pentagram that the worshippers shall drink of it. Before our God and Goddess, we shall consume and be consumed by the wine of wisdom and blessing. Before the Lord and the Lady, we shall consume the cakes and the wine. Before Zarach and Zaruna."

The Cakes & Wine Ceremony

The cakes and wine are placed upon the altar. The High Priestess goes to the altar and then turns to face the High Priest who has followed her. He may kiss her feet, knees and stretch out his arms in a gesture of adoration, or he may simply hold out his hands in a gesture of petition and say: *"Before our secret queen, Zaruna, lady of the night, give blessing on this food that it will bring us fulfilment of all that we desire."*

The High Priestess replies: *"The secret blessing is given."*

The High Priest takes the cup of wine and offers it to the High Priestess. She takes up her athamé and places the point in the cup, saying: *"Health, joy, strength, peace, love. These are the gifts of those whom we follow, Zarach and Zaruna."*

The High Priestess lays the athame on the altar. She takes the cup in both hands and drinks. Then she offers the cup to the High Priest. The High Priest takes the plate of cakes and holds them out. The High Priestess blesses each cake with the moistened blade of the athamé. She then cuts one cake in half and shares it with the High Priest. He distributes the cakes to the other coven members and returns the plate. He bows or kisses and adores.

The Invocation of the God

The High Priest stands before the altar facing the South. In one hand he holds the sword and in the other he holds the wand. The High Priestess faces him carrying her wand with which she invokes, saying: *"Giver of Life and strength, Giver of Plenty, Witch Lord Zarach, thou who art also Lord of the path of death and peace, Descend. I call thee unto the body of thy servant and priest ... "*

Using the wand, the High Priestess draws the Pentagram sunwise upon the body of the High Priest. This is followed by the five-fold salute.

All the coven members bow.

The Invocation of the Goddess

The High Priestess stands before the altar, facing South. In one hand she carries the athamé, and in the other she carries the cup, (or sometimes the scourge). The High Priest faces her, bearing the wand with which he invokes, saying:

"I invoke and call upon thee, Threefold Goddess of the moon, Zaruna of the secret name. Queen of the moonlit sea, fairer than the night and silver clad, thee I invoke. Mother of the Moon and the calm waters, let thy light fall upon us, for thy hair is a pool of stars in the darkness. I call upon thee. Widow of the waning moon whose children have grown and left thee to sorrow, guard us with learning and grant us a place in thy dark cloak of understanding. Thee I invoke. Descend, I call thee, unto the body of thy servant and priestess... "

The High Priest draws the sign of the pentagram sunwise upon the body of the High Priestess. This is followed by the five-fold salute.

This ceremony is frequently known as 'Drawing Down the Moon'. References to it by this name appear in many newspaper clippings and occult fiction books.

The Charge

Hear now the words of the Great Mother who has been called un-numbered names. Hear now the counsel of Zaruna, for she has said, I have been with you from the beginning of time and I shall be with you beyond its ending, for I am Time. You shall come to me in silence, for I know all of your needs and desires.

You shall gather before me, openly or secretly, by day or by night. I am your Queen and I only, yet to my faithful servants I have taught much wisdom, if you will endure.

To those who follow not the secret ways, you shall conceal from them the secrets of your wisdom. But strive to deal with them fairly, for there are many who worship me in some other name, and many know me not.

Keep unsullied your own ideals and yet respect the ideals of other people. Many mortals strive for worthy greatness and their lives are touched with glory.

Grant to your friends within the Craft and without the Craft, your love and best words and cheer. Betray them not but give them only happiness at your hands.

Seek not quarrels and warfare, not for any reason. Such reasons as there are for warfare are mostly born of fantasies and fears. Rather seek out reasons for a mutual respect and enjoy together the manifold possibilities of life.

Seek out spiritual strength and counsel that you shall not be overwhelmed by sudden misfortunes.

Be gentle with your body and not severe, for I have given you your body as a gift and you are my own child. Nor seek to maim the body of your foe for I have created him, also.

Keep peace within yourself and hold honour dearly in your own heart, for this is the way of peace unto me.

Feign not affection, nor love where there is no love. Part willingly from those who are a vexation unto you.

Fear not the passing of the years, for there is wisdom not in my youthful countenance, but in my darker face. Fear not life, for you shall remember that the wheel of death and rebirth shall level all

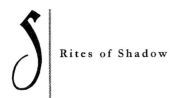

things in the end.

Fear not death, for as you are my own true servant, I shall enfold you in my cloak and you shall sleep until another dawn.

My servant, remember that though this world shall seem a place of sadness and evil, corruption and devastation, yet I have made this world most beautiful, and you also.

Therefore accept that which life shall bring to you. Live it and know all of my beauty.

For know that I am she that spun this world. I am the changeless and ever changing goddess, Zaruna, Queen of Heaven. I am she who is crowned with the stars. My cloak covers all men and my voice is the whisper of the midnight winds.

O my beloved servant, come to me secretly. Worship me in silence and I will bring you multitudes of blessings. Whatever life shall bring to you, I promise you ecstasy in an ending of all desire. Call, therefore, upon the name of Zaruna, your Queen and you shall come to me.

The Ceremony for Candlemas

Strictly speaking this is a ceremony for women, and men may or may not be invited in. The women set out the circle and prepare it with early spring flowers if possible. They light the lamps or candles and invoke the Goddess to come to them. They welcome her and install her, possibly on a special 'throne' which has been decorated for the festival.

They deal with any business which cannot be done when men are present. After this, the High Priestess asks whether the men shall be permitted to enter. If the women decide in favour of the men, then the men are called in to adore the Goddess and to hear some secret of women's magic. Cakes and wine may be distributed and feasting and dancing may end the festival.

The Candlemas invocation (Spoken by the High Priestess)
"Queen and Lady, Zaruna of the Night.... Secret Goddess - thy servants call upon thee for this is the time of thy festival. Come now and honour our circle. Enter, Maiden, come now to thy throne and bless thy servants. Come. Come. Come."

Later the High Priestess says: *"This is the festival of womankind and the night of the Goddess whom we worship, the Lady, the Moon, Zaruna. Yet the goddess alone is without her consort and her presence in this place does not mean that the God is no more. The menfolk are without on this night. How say you, servants of Zaruna, shall we let them enter?"*

The assembled women then decide whether the men should be allowed to join the circle. In practice they always decide in favour but if, for some reason, the men are vetoed for the night, then it is up to the High Priestess to deal with any other magic and formally close the ceremony.

The Spring Equinox

The ceremony of the spring equinox calls for flowers and greenery decorating the altar. The purpose behind the ritual is to entreat the Lady to bless new-born animals and crops. The High Priestess blesses unsown seed. The wine is blessed and that which is not drunk is poured on to the fields or the earth. Today the bonfire is likely to be a token one, i.e. a special candle. The wine is likely to be poured on to the front garden. Leaping dances are out of the question in most flats but the rejoicing ceremony remains the same.

The Spring Invocation
"Hear ye servants of our Lady Queen, Zaruna, and know that this is the time that the Goddess is renewed in all of her glory. She is beauteous and young once more. Tall and graceful, she walks among us as a maiden and our beloved one. Come, our fairest lady. Grant blessing unto the seeds which become the flowers of tomorrow. Come, O gracious lady, and protect that which is newly

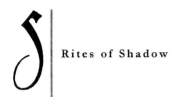

born, that children and animals may grow strong beneath thy hands. Let the seed be blessed in Thy Name, O Zaruna. Let the wine be blessed which is the wine of spring and the wine of the Queen. Let the seed be cast unto the earth. Let the fire of joy be lit and let the wine be shared."

The men of the coven take the seeds from the High Priestess and throw it outside the circle. The High Priestess blesses the wine and her women pass it around the circle. The High Priest lights the 'bonfire', which is a signal for the party to begin.

May Eve

This isn't really a working ceremony at all. It is a celebration of the fact that the God and the Goddess are lovers who bring forth the new crops and so on. Ideally it requires a site with a May Pole, a marvellous party laid on and an all-night session in the woods. In practice, the High Priest represents the God and he moves about the circle seeking for the Goddess. When the High Priestess is found, she is dressed up with flowers, ribbons and perfume, for the Goddess was the original May Queen.

The High Priest says: *"I bless the crops and animals. I bless the seeds and the roots. I bless the stems and the buds. I bless the coming of life in plants, and in animals and in children. In the Name of Zarach."*

The High Priestess says: *"I bless the new growth and the new born. I bless the seeds and the roots. I bless the coming of life in plants, and in animals and in children. In the Name of Zaruna."*

They turn to each other and say together, *"God and Goddess, Blessed be."*

The party lasts for the rest of the evening. [And would my local vicar please note that placing the May Pole inside his Christian church was not really a good idea. Nor would his pretty little May Queen have been a virgin by the end of the evening!]

The Summer Solstice

The cauldron is placed before the altar. It is filled with water and decorated with summer flowers. Coven members stand around the circle, men and women alternately. The High Priest stands in the North and the High Priestess faces him in the South where she invokes the sun.

"Lord of Heaven and Power of the Sun. We invoke thee in the secret name of Zarach, O Lord of Greatest Light. Now is the time of your glory and power. Place, we implore, your shield between us and all powers of darkness. Shoot forth your arrows of light to protect us. Grant us at this time green fields and good hunting. Give to your servants orchards of fullness and corn that has risen high. Show us within the time of splendour the pathway to the place of the Lord and the Lady."

The High Priestess draws a pentagram above the altar. She plunges the tip of her wand into the cauldron, withdraws it and holds it upright, saying: *"The knife to the cup, the wand to the cauldron, the sun to the earth but the flesh to the spirit."*

The High Priest then salutes the High Priestess and speaks words of ancient wisdom as follows:

"Now is the time of the sun in its glory when our Lord Zarach is at his height in the heavens. Yet it must also be remembered that now is the time of Zarach's decline to his death and rebirth at the darkest time in winter. As it is with the God, so is it also with man. We also journey throughout our time from birth unto death and to rebirth upon our way. We must remember that the goddess Zaruna will raise the God with the kiss of rebirth and send him yet again upon his journey. We also go down into the cloak of Zaruna's darkness and her veils hide us from mortal sight. But the tomb is the womb of time from which we return to other lives, to share once more the knowledge and the love of our fellows and our friends."

The High Priestess then says: *"Dance, one and all. Dance about the cauldron of the Craft. Be blessed by the waters of Zaruna that are contained in the cauldron, and remember that which you have heard this night."*

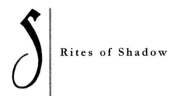

The coven dances three times around the circle whilst the High Priestess sprinkles them all with water. This is followed by initiations, cakes and wine. etc.

August Eve

The Lammas eve ceremony is the converse of the Candlemass one. The men proceed to the circle and set it up on their own. The High Priest invokes the God and any exclusive masculine magic gets done at this stage. The men are reminded of the fact that the coven women are waiting and may, or may not, be invited in for the occasion. If the women are permitted to enter, then they will be taught some secret of hunting magic and reminded that the God's death is, in itself, a promise of rebirth.

Lammas Invocation (Done by the High Priest)

"Lord of the Sun, the Hunt and the Fire, Zarach, be with us now before the time of departure. We call upon thee this night, for this is the time of Thy festival. Come, before the time of departure is upon us, come and bless this rite."

Later, the High Priest says: *"This is the festival of man, the hunt and the harvest which provides for the time of darkness. Yet the God stands alone and without his proper consort. She must grieve for his departure and take him to the dark place. The women folk have been excluded on this night. How say you, servants of Zarach, shall we let them enter?"*

If it is decided against the women entering, then the men must complete their ceremony and close the ritual of their own accord, but this very seldom happens.

It is far more likely that the women will be called in to witness that the God Zarach is now dying, but even in his death he gives strength to the grain, life to the harvest and so on. Initiations can be held. Cakes and wine will be shared before the festival ends.

The Autumn Equinox

The altar is decorated with autumn leaves, ears of corn, pine cones and so on. The ceremony serves a double purpose: First to thank the Lord and the Lady for their bounty, much like a harvest festival. However, because it is autumn, the Lord is barely present and the feast is also our hope for his rebirth. The High Priest stands west of the altar and the High Priestess in the East.

High Priest: "*We are met at this time to give thanks to the God and the Goddess for that which we have received throughout the year. We have harvested their gifts and stored away the food for the time of darkness that is soon to be upon us. I ask and implore that Zarach shall bless the seed corn that is ours for the coming year for, although the god is in darkness, we will remember that he will come again.*"

High Priestess: "*Zarach, we call upon you, our hidden God who goes through the realm of death to gain life and rebirth and youth. Zarach, our God, and Zaruna our Queen, accept our thanks for the gifts which you have given us in this year. Preserve us in the dark days when food is scarce. Keep from us the threat of famine. Give us hope throughout the night for Zarach has gone to the place of death. Mother Goddess, Zaruna, Dark Queen, let Zarach return to us, his people. Zaruna, death goddess, in you is all the future. Goddess most gentle - let the fire be lit to celebrate our faith in the return.*"

The High Priest salutes the High Priestess, who lights the fire. She holds her rod to the skies and says: "*The Goddess hears. Zaruna answers. The wheel of night and day spins on and the Lord will return to us. Let this bring rejoicing.*"

The High Priestess leads the dancing. Initiations follow. The cakes and wine are handed around and any other business is dealt with before the party ends.

Samhain or Hallowe'en

Hallowe'en is a joyful ceremony and it marks the end and the beginning of the Craft year. Ideally, one should proceed to the ritual dancing the whole way, riding a broomstick and carrying a torch. Whatever the customs of the past, the ceremony today is more frequently held indoors. Orange candles are used, though occasionally black ones are also put out because they are in keeping with 'the feast of the living and the dead'.

Like other ceremonies, this one starts with a prayer for protection against unbelievers. There is a 'Call to the Dead', that those who were of the coven, those who are and those who will be of the coven shall join the meeting. There is a brief silence before the Moon Goddess is invoked. A cup of wine is blessed in the name of the Dark Mother and those whom she governs. The meeting is then opened for a general discussion on future policy. Initiations may be held and feasting follows with dancing.

According to one school of thought, it is considered discourteous to dismiss the dead guests. In practice a 'Farewell' is often given, just before dawn, and the wine is poured out on to the ground as the candles are extinguished.

The prayer for protection is quoted elsewhere.

Call To The Dead

"Harken to the voice of our souls and hear us, ye who wander. Harken, for we call upon those who have passed from this life, back through the generations of man to the time of our first parents. We light the beacon so that you are guided to this place and we call upon you. Listen to the voices of our souls, all those of the past. Harken unto us, those who shall be of our house. The gulf between the worlds is narrow at this time. Approach, all those who were of the Craft. Come, those who will be of the Craft, come and share our joy this night. Let the Cup be filled in the name of the Three, for we would speak once more to those who have passed from us, and we will see those who are yet to be. Come to us and rejoice."

Invocation To The Moon

"Zaruna, Queen of the midnight skies, we rejoice in thy blessing. We call upon thy maiden beauty to bless us with insight and serenity. We invoke thy silver graciousness to light the ways of lovers and to guard the sleep of children. We call upon thy dark aspect this night, lady of the dead and the unborn. Cast back thy cloak and grant to us the sight of those who are passed and those who are to be. Show us in this darkness thine understanding. Grant us, Zaruna, thy blessing."

Blessing of the Wine

"Zaruna, Dark Queen, bless the wine in this cup in token of the cauldron which contained three drops of wisdom for all the world. Creatures of earth and creatures of water, creatures of air and creatures of fire, friends in life and friends in death! Gather here in the Dark Queen's name ere she gathers earth unto her again."

Dance

> *Power of stone and power of earth,*
> *Power that shapes our place of birth,*
> *Spin the wheel of night and day,*
> *Spin the wheel, Or-Ah-Ay.*
> *Power of ice and water free,*
> *Power that hides the depths of sea,*
> *Weave the web of night and day,*
> *Spin the wheel, Or-Ah-Ay.*
> *Power of wind and power of air,*
> *Power of mountains bleak and bare,*
> *Turn the time of night and day,*
> *Spin the wheel, Or-Ah-Ay.*
> *Power of flame and power of fire,*
> *Power of all our vast desire,*
> *Light of dark and light of day,*
> *Spin the wheel, Or-Ah-Ay.*

The Farewell Before Dawn

"Friends of today, friends of yesteryear and friends that are yet to be, we have met and rejoiced this night in our knowledge that time is no barrier and that friendship endures. Yet the hours of our feast draw to their close and time brings this feast to an end. Therefore go to your appointed places, disturbing not those who would fear you, nor harming any substance of this world. Remember that we will meet again some other Hallows Eve.

"So let it end with love and blessing on us all."

Yule—The Winter Solstice

The cauldron of the Craft is placed in the centre of the circle. It should be placed over a fire of wood gathered by all members of the coven. The wood represents all that was dark, evil and old and all that one would like to be rid of. In due course it will be destroyed by fire. The lights are extinguished and the fire is lit. From the fire, candles are lit and those within the circle begin the dance which denotes the strengthening of light and life from the darkest time of the year.

In practice, few Yule ceremonies are ever worked out of doors. Very often, the cauldron contains the bits and pieces for the fire instead of boiling over the flames. The occasion is one of rejoicing, followed by a feast.

Incantation

> *Queen of Heaven, moon and night,*
> *Water, air and fire and earth,*
> *Widowed queen, return the one,*
> *Bring the Light unto its birth,*
> *Queen of sadness, grieving, woe,*
> *Queen of future, queen of bane,*
> *Queen that guards the new and past,*

Grant that Light return again.
Rise, O child and new beginning,
Show thy light to all the world,
Light above the land and ocean,
Be the veil of darkness furled.
Blessed be the triple Mother,
Queen of dark and queen of day,
Hers the dance and hers rejoicing,
Ap-Ap-An-O-Ir-Ut-Ay.

This invocation is followed by initiations, if any, and cakes and wine etc.

The First Initiation

The circle is set up with everything in its proper place. Prayers for protection are made and any secret business that the candidate is not permitted to see is dealt with, for the candidate is not in the room. If the ceremony is held out of doors, then the candidate must be far enough away to neither see nor hear what is happening. The Circle is opened by placing two lighted white candles in the West. These candles mark the 'Gateway'.

The High Priestess spreads out her hands over the Circle at this point and delegates a messenger to bring the candidate to the edge of the Circle. The messenger brings the candidate and place him just outside the Circle facing the High Priestess, then the messenger returns to his proper place in the Circle.

High Priestess: *"Seeker, you have moved through life unto this place. Know that if you come within this Circle, you have departed from the normal world of men. You have heard of dread domains and strange perils, of terrible fates and awesome beings. Know that there is still time to turn back. You may go from this place without*

one word of reproach, no blame, no loss of courage. Will you choose to go back now?"

Candidate: *"I will not go back."*

[If the candidate decides against joining the Craft at this point he is free to go and you never discuss his reasons for going, nor do you mention the Craft to him ever again.]

High Priestess: *"Then come within the circle of your own free will, no one assisting you in any way. Stand where I shall indicate.* [The West side of the altar.] *Be the God and the Goddess witnesses that you have entered this place of your own free will, fairly warned beforehand of that which might follow. What seek you in this place?"*

Candidate: *"I seek the path of the wise, the secret learning before the sign of the Craft."*

High Priestess: *"The secret learning is not lightly given, yet with study it is yours. The sign of the Craft is the sign of the Pentagram. Know that this is our shield against the outside world. The Pentagram is also the star that we follow. The Pentagram is that on which we swear an oath unto the Craft."*

Candidate: *"I would swear that oath."*

High Priestess: *"Think before you swear, for the oath of the Craft is not an easy promise to stand by. It has brought to those bound by it pain and suffering in the past. It has brought torture and death to many who were only suspected of practising its mysteries. Remember the Burning Time when all we could promise our associates was a painless death before the flames took hold. Do you still desire to take that oath, knowing that what has been may well be again?"*

Candidate: *"I will take the oath."*

High Priestess*:* *"Put your right hand upon this symbol and your left hand in mine. Now say after me:*

"Before the Lord and the Lady, I ..... do of my own will most solemnly swear to keep secret the knowledge of the Craft which shall be given unto me. I swear before the God and the Goddess that I will not betray my associates in the Craft, however greatly I am tempted or tortured to do so. I swear before the Lord and the Lady that I will not use the knowledge I am given in any evil manner to cause trouble to my fellow men. I will hold my knowledge secret still, save to my associates in the Craft. This do I swear before Zarach and Zaruna. So mote it be."

High Priestess: [Touching the candidate's forehead and hands with charged oil]: *"With oil I consecrate you Priest and Witch.* [Touching the same with water]: *With water I consecrate you Priest and Witch.* [Picking up a candle and moving it through the sign of the Pentagram]: *With fire, I consecrate you Priest and Witch."*

All: *"New-made Witch, I salute you."*
High Priestess: *"It is our tradition that in this hour you choose a new name by which your associates shall know you. Many have chosen the names of great practitioners who have gone from hence, but this is by no means essential. Speak now of your new name."*

Candidate: *"My new name is ....."*

The High Priestess repeats the name and then everyone else repeats it after her. High Priestess: *"Candidate, the gifts of the Lord and the Lady are multitudinous blessings, and in token of this we will give you a gift in this hour. Receive therefore this athamé which we have made in our circle. This is the weapon of a Witch and,*

using this, you shall fashion things considered by the ignorant to be magic. Keep this weapon with you at all times. Let none other touch it lest they harm your own being. With this athamé you are as you are made this night, Priest and Witch.

"Use your athamé to cut and fashion your own wand of magic to your desire, for that is yours to do and none may help you in that task.

"Use your athamé to engrave the sign of the Pentagram, for this shall be a shield against rebellious spirits.

"You are familiar with other tools upon the Altar of the Craft. You see the cup of the Goddess, the burning incense and the candles which light our pathway. Take now the Witch cord that I give to you and wear it as a new insignia. Now, stand where I shall indicate." [In front of the altar].

"Mighty Ones of the world above, know that ..... is a Priest and Witch before Zarach and Zaruna.

"Mighty Ones of the World below, know that ..... is a Priest and Witch before Zarach and Zaruna.

"Mighty Ones of the Eastern Quarter, know that ..... is a Priest and Witch before Zarach and Zaruna.

"Mighty Ones of the Southern Quarter, know that ..... is a Priest and Witch before Zarach and Zaruna.

"Mighty Ones of the Western Quarter, know that ..... is a Priest and Witch before Zarach and Zaruna.

Mighty Ones of the Northern Quarter, know that ..... is a Priest and Witch before Zarach and Zaruna.

..... before Zarach and Zaruna I salute you."

This is one form of Craft initiation. It is fair to say that there are other forms. Some of them call for a purification by scourging. Some of them call for intercourse. Undoubtedly some of the 'initiations' that we have come across have been physically harmful to the candidates themselves for the scourging has marked them all the days of their lives. Some of these so-called rituals have provided a new line in pornography, complete with 'blue films' afterwards.

Many covens insist that the candidate should be ritually bound and barely able to hobble into the Circle. Others prefer the candidate to be bound before the scourging takes place. The more responsible Craft members seem to feel that a candidate must enter freely and that joining must be the candidate's choice. Being led into the Circle by the end of a rope with ankles bound is the wrong thing to do.

Never join a coven on impulse; think carefully beforehand. They should likewise think carefully before they let you join them. Ask if nudity, scourging or intercourse are a part of their working. Nudity is a question that has been debated in Witchcraft circles for years, and is used by a minority of Craft members. Scourging should not be used. It can cause grievous bodily harm and, on occasions, the 'witches' who use scourging have vanished into the night with a crop of interesting pictures and left a totally bewildered candidate behind. Craft members loathe this sort of thing because it stirs up public opinion against the sincere Craft members. Ritual intercourse is left up to individual Coven members to decide on. It does NOT turn up in a first initiation ceremony. Do not join the 'coven' that insists that it does.

Remember, never join on impulse. Take time and think about it carefully.

Initiation - Second Degree

The circle is set up and the altar prepared. When all is ready, the High Priestess turns to the candidate.

High Priestess: *"Stand where I shall indicate.* [Before the altar.] *Mighty Ones of the world above, know that ..... is now prepared to be made a High Priest of Zarach and Zaruna.*

"Mighty Ones of the world below, know that ..... is now prepared to be made a High Priest of Zarach and Zaruna.

"Mighty Ones of the Eastern Quarter, know that ..... is now prepared to be made a High Priest of Zarach and Zaruna.

"Mighty Ones of the Southern Quarter, know that ..... is now prepared to be made a High Priest of Zarach and Zaruna.

"Mighty Ones of the Western Quarter, know that ..... is now prepared to be made a High Priest of Zarach and Zaruna.

"Mighty Ones of the Northern Quarter, know that ..... is now prepared to be made a High Priest of Zarach and Zaruna.

"....., speak now before the God and the Goddess who weigh your most secret heart. State first what you have done with your knowledge of the Craft."

Candidate: *"I have guarded my knowledge from the profane who would dishonour that knowledge. I have sought to further my own studies with the help of my fellow Craft members. I have kept secret the rituals and ceremonies of the God and the Goddess, nor have I spoken their secret names to any man. I have kept faith with my fellow Craft members and betrayed them not to their enemies. This I swore to do and this I have done."*

High Priestess: *"What do you seek within the next degree?"*

Candidate: *"I seek to better serve the Lord and the Lady."*

High Priestess: *"It is said that the Craft is a way of power, yet before power is given, there is an oath to be sworn."*

Candidate: *"I can but swear that which I have sworn before, not to betray my secrets, nor my associates. I honour the God Zarach and the Goddess Zaruna and this I will swear, that I serve them as the Lord and the Lady. They will see into my soul and know of truth. If I am faithful to them, the Lord and the Lady shall be my reward. If I am faithless, then the years are long before I shall find them out*

again. If I am too daring, then Zarach and Zaruna will turn from me and, in that moment, destroy me."
High Priestess: *"You have called destruction upon yourself if you are unworthy of this degree. The God and the Goddess are your judges.* [Pause] *Destruction is withheld. Therefore do I consecrate you with the earth at your feet, for you are and shall remain a child of the earth, though you follow the God and the Goddess.*

"I consecrate you with water, that it shall symbolise all your desire in the time to come.

"I consecrate you with air, that it shall be your will to worship Zarach and Zaruna unto all your days.

"I consecrate you with fire, that you shall be a light to your fellow Craft members for all of their days, working as a High Priest before Zarach and Zaruna. Be the God and the Goddess my witnesses in this hour that ..... shall be a High Priest before ye."

The High Priestess turns to the altar and rests her hands upon it, invoking all her strength and blessing from the Goddess. After a pause, she turns, places her hands on the shoulders of the candidate and says: *"Unto thee be the power. This do I will."*

Candidate: *"Let blessing be."*

High Priestess: *"I consecrate thee by the earth which bears the path your feet must travel.*

"I consecrate thee by the water which is love and secret knowledge.

"I consecrate thee by the air which is a will to magical power.

"I consecrate thee by the fire which cleanses all things

"Above that which is below do I consecrate thee.

"Below that which is above do I consecrate thee, High Priest and Witch before the Lord and the Lady."

[Some covens insist that the candidate now scourges the High Priestess at this point. After that, one of the traditional Craft legends is acted out. Sometimes this is the story of the Goddess

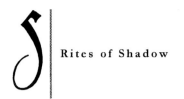

seeking out the God through the underworld. Sometimes it is a more modern story of Craft history with the emphasis on the Craft in the world today. An ancient story will involve an official Narrator and coven members mime their parts with the newly-made High Priest also taking a part in the story. A modern story, i.e. the story of the Witches who stopped Adolf Hitler and aided the D-day invasion of France with their phantom fleet will probably be by narration only. Done properly in the right atmosphere, this can be a very telling experience. The Narrator finishes with the words, *"For this is a tale of our people and now it is ended.."*]

Candidate: *"You have told a tale of yesterday, yet we still have to weave the tales of tomorrow. For tomorrow is mist and moonlight only. It is a tale with less substance than dreams and tomorrow is hidden away within the breath of the Goddess. It is we who shall make it real."*

High Priestess: *"Hear ye, Dwellers in the world above and know that ... is a consecrated High Priest before the God and the Goddess.*

"Hear ye, Dwellers in the world below and know that ..... is a consecrated High Priest before the God and the Goddess.

"Hear ye, Dwellers in the Eastern Quarter and know that ..... is a consecrated High Priest before the God and the Goddess.

"Hear ye, Dwellers in the Southern Quarter and know that .... is a consecrated High Priest before the God and the Goddess.

"Hear ye, Dwellers in the Western Quarter and know that ..... is a consecrated High Priest before the God and the Goddess.

"Hear ye, Dwellers in the Northern Quarter and know that ....is a consecrated High Priest before the God and the Goddess.

"Let blessing be."

Note:- Not all covens recognise three degrees. Some covens work their own promotions based on different theories. They also gif different titles. Be a little wary if someone introduces themselves as 'The Absolute Pandjandrum of the Witches'- grand titles were never really our style!

The Third Degree (or so-called Great Rite)

There is a lot of misunderstanding about this particular ritual. If you believe the newspapers, or the writers of occult fiction, you might be forgiven for assuming that this is the 'Black Mass' and that it is all very weird and horrible. Nonetheless the 'Great Rite' is probably the oldest of all magical rituals, common to mankind the world over. Even today it is used (and sometimes abused), by Craft members, magicians of all types and varieties, and plenty of other people in the 'occult world'.

The idea behind the Great Rite is that of asking the God and the Goddess to aid in the conception of a leader of men; it might be a tribal king or the next High Priest, or some other very special soul. Obviously the conception of the next hero was far too important to be left to chance. Such a hero might be called upon to lead the tribe to the Happy Lands where game was plentiful, the land where rivers ran with wine and no man oppressed another, or whatever sort of heaven you needed. The mother of such a hero was chosen with great care.

The child was conceived at the right time for magic and destiny. Sometimes the High Priest played the part of the God. Sometimes the Priestess took the part of the Goddess. Either way, the child so conceived was regarded as a very special entity. Where the Craft was concerned, the magical child was the responsibility of the Coven who were bound to support the child and the mother to their utmost ability. Born into the Craft in such a manner, the child had no need of initiations and tests. He stood in a special position as a super-human who, in childhood, must be cared for and defended against evil, if necessary with the lives of the other coven members.

Used in its original form, the ritual is primitive, but it is effective. Obviously much depends on what sort of child you ask for: asking for a child who will lead the children of men into an age of peace is surely a laudable intention. Asking for a mighty warrior who will saturate the land with the blood of his enemies is not such a great idea.

The ritual described above is sometimes referred to as 'The Rite of Tanith'. It is confused with the Black Mass, though it has *nothing* to do with the Black Mass, which is simply the ordinary Mass read backwards and shouldn't have a girl on the altar anyway!

The Great Rite is also confused with the 'Mass of Saint Secairie'. This is a ceremony purporting to involve magical intercourse between a Catholic priest and a woman in order to cause trouble or death. The stories of this ceremony appear to originate in the late Middle Ages. I have been unable to trace an authentic ritual by this name, but one must take into account the environment of the Middle Ages, a time of superstition and a time when various members of the priesthood were hated as money-grubbers whose celibacy was, at best, dubious.

Undoubtedly those within the monasteries were better off than most of the peasants. Moreover physically healthy men in a monastery were still vulnerable to temptation. Under such circumstances a priest might well take his mistress to a desolate place, but probably more out of biological need rather than any dirty magical work! Nonetheless the legend grew up, and the whisper that 'he had been seen working the Mass of Saint Secairie' was enough to cause a priest a fair amount of trouble.

Occult fiction writers have combined factors from all three ceremonies in books that deal with Witches and black magicians. Not surprisingly, this has confused the general public. To add to the confusion, occult fiction writers insist that this sort of thing must be done in the ruins of a desecrated church with the climax occurring on the stroke of midnight.

But consider the early Christians. Saint Augustine was advised to build Christian churches on pagan holy spots and amalgamate the pagan gods with Christian saints. Not surprisingly, the pagans still regarded those holy spots as their own, although there was a new temple to a strange God within the holy wood or on top of the sacred hill. It would cause no end of trouble to be found working a ritual in your ancient holy place during the day, so when could you use your traditional holy spot without detection? Obviously in the middle of the night when all good Christian people were supposed to be asleep in their beds.

So long as the pagans were home again by cock-crow, no one would be any the wiser and the ancient gods would still be happy with their worshippers. If the church had fallen into disuse so much the better, for there would be less chance of interruption by a sleepy and furious priest. One must allow for the fact that the pagans had a point of view - even if one does not share that viewpoint.

However, just occasionally the secret gatherings of the Craft and other groups did get overlooked by outsiders. Non-initiates are not the best people to describe what is going on in any magical ceremony. They would neither see what was going on clearly, nor would they hear all the words of the ritual. Moreover they would probably be scared stiff at the thought of what these folks would do if discovered in their secret rituals. Consequently some of the reporting is highly suspect, to say the very least. Small wonder that the Craft members had a name for wholesale orgies and so on.

To be absolutely fair, this country escaped most of the Witchcraft persecutions. For a very great deal of our history, the penalty for practising witchcraft was six hours in the stocks and/or a year in prison. The death penalty was given when high treason was suspected, or when death by poison was involved. Treason meant death by fire, but the poison penalty was a different matter. Poison was something that not many people understood. Some of the symptoms were known, but proving poison without today's forensic science was a serious problem. Nobody could say with certainty what the poison was. Nobody could say with certainty who had

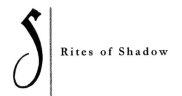

prepared the poison, which is not the same thing as saying who administered it.

Poison was supposed to be something that Witches knew about and, to be fair, the Craft members probably knew more about the plants, herbs and toxic vegetation than anyone else. The death penalty for poisoning was understandable in the circumstances and it follows the original Biblical command, 'Thou shalt not suffer a dealer in poisons to live'. (Oh, you've only read the translation 'Thou shalt not suffer a Witch to live'. I'm sorry, but there was no Hebrew word for 'Witch'. The original word was 'dealer in poisons'. A tribal civilisation in pre-scientific days couldn't afford to have a dealer in poisons around. He might go mad and poison the well, in which case the tribe would all die. A dealer in poisons was too much of a liability. You had to execute him before he killed everyone else! The translation into the word 'Witch' has caused grief and suffering throughout all Europe.)

But the Witches of today are not usually blamed for poison. They are blamed for orgies, 'the Black Mass' and so on.

Here, for the first time, is the Witches Great Rite written out in full:
The coven assembles and the circle is prepared. The prayer for protection is chanted and the circle is worked. Cakes and wine are handed around. Then everyone who is not sufficiently advanced in the Craft is sent away. The altar is moved out of the Circle if necessary.

The High Priestess then addresses the man and the woman, reminding them that this must be their own choice. If they elect proper intercourse before the Powers, then it must be a wholehearted committal for a magical child, not just a private party under rather unusual conditions. The decision is left entirely to the two people involved and, with these words, the High Priestess departs. Everyone else who has remained goes with her, leaving the couple to themselves.

Left alone together, the woman gives the man the ancient five-fold salute and, possibly, a ritual scourging. He returns the same. The man then 'draws down the moon' on the woman's body. In theory they then decide whether to do the Great Rite completely, or in token only.

The decision having been taken, the woman then lies down in the centre of the Circle with her head towards the North. The man stands at her feet.

Woman: *"I am she who is called Zaruna by men who desire me. That which I represent is yours, for I give pleasure and love most freely. Only be pure of heart and body and soul if you would know that which I am."*

Man: *"I am desirous of your gifts and I come to honour you. Seeking the love of the Goddess, I come to receive your gifts."*

Woman: *"In this moment, come."*

The man goes down to her and covers her body with his own. If the intercourse is a token one only, that is all that happens. Otherwise they both lie perfectly still so as not to excite each other. It is essential to come to the end of the following speech before orgasm is reached.

Woman: *"I am the joy of the earth, but unto my children I am also the ecstasy of the spirit. Mine is the Law of Love, for I am the joy in the heart of a man. I am Goddess of all life and my love moves through existence. I am all Beauty. I am all Desire. I am beloved of the God and all mankind. I am she whom you seek in this hour and yet I was with you before the dawn of time and I shall enfold you at time's ending. I am the end of all desire. Let blessing be."*

Man: *"Let blessing be."*

After a short interval, the Great Rite being over, the two celebrants of the Great Rite rise in silence. The senior of the pair ends the ceremony and closes the Circle, putting out candles and so on. They then robe and join the others. Later that evening there may be some form of presentation, a snakeskin garter for the girl, possibly a magical sword for the man.

The 'Great Rite' is not used by every Witch coven, indeed many covens would throw up their hands in horror at the thought of it! Other covens, intent on staying within the morals of the land, allow this only between married couples. Other covens again insist that the private lives of Witches and outsiders belong in the bedroom and not in a magic circle at all. Contrary to the Sunday newspapers, opinion on this ceremony is deeply divided within the Craft.

It is to be hoped that this book will clear up some of the misunderstandings and bring more tolerance between the Craft and the outside world. If so, I have not dared a coven's death curse in vain.

In conclusion

As explained in the interview with the author at the beginning of this book, the original *The Devil's Prayerbook* was written in an attempt to prevent a more sinister publication from appearing on the market. Although the rituals were contrived for the purpose they were penned by a genuine Witch who was determined not to give away real Craft secrets.

Nevertheless, these are workable rituals with an authentic background and are derived from genuine Craft traditions. The chants and rituals were taken up by newcomers wishing to establish new covens and (since most Witches are eclectic gatherers of spells and rituals) incorporated either in whole or in part into already existing coven workings. As a result, many have become established, by their repeated use, as part of traditional Wiccan worship.

It must also be noted that since *The Devil's Praybook* has been around since 1972, the author's rituals and invocations can now be considered older than quite a considerable amount of other modern Wiccan writing.

In its present form, *Rites of Shadow* incorporates an exact copy of the original text, plus additional material from the author's own personal working books.

Glossary

Adept–a master of the magical arts, an experienced practitioner.

Astral– as in 'astral plans' or 'astral travel', refers to alternate dimensions and interaction with them.

Athamé–a Witch's personal ceremonial knife.

Autumn Equinox– festival also known as Modron.

Balefire–also known as Wendfire or Needfire. Ritual bonfire created in a special way and usually kindled with special woods with religious and/or magical significance.

Banishing–to magically get rid of something, usually unwanted or inappropriate energies. The magical or spiritual cleansing of an object or place is also known as 'banishing'.

The Black Mass–nothing to do with Witches or Witchcraft, this is a perversion of the Christian Eucharist.

Book of Shadows–a Witch's personal book of notes, spells and rituals.

Candalmas–festival also known as Imbolc, Oimelc, or the Feast of Brigid held 2nd February.

The Charge–a speech supposed to have been given originally by the Goddess and handed down from Priestess to Priestess.

Charm–spoken or chanted words of magical intent. Can be another word for a spell.

Consecration–the magical or spiritual preparation and 'programming' of an object or area.

Coven– a group of Witches, for practical purposes and tradition this usually has no more than thirteen members.

The Craft–a shortened form of 'Witchcraft', used by insiders.

Deosil– 'with the sun': movements made in a clockwise direction.

Degrees– there are three degrees which denote rank within the Craft.

Divination–magical or psychic methods of inquiry.

Drawing Down the Moon– invocation to Lunar or Goddess energies, and their expression through the presiding Priestess.

Esbat–the regular non-festival meetings of a coven.

The Great Rite— the symbolic conjoining of male and female energies. This may include private sexual intercourse between the two participants, but usually is enacted in symbol only.

High Priest, High Priestess—the leaders of a Witches' group.

Invocation—the calling, summoning or beseeching of a deity or spirit.

Lammas—festival also known as August Eve since held on or around 31st July, also known as Lughnassadh.

Magic—the ritual use of psychic powers and energies.

Magic Circle—the ritually prepared area, or temple, usually circular in layout.

May Eve—festival known as Walpurgis Night or Beltane.

Neophyte— one newly accepted into the Craft—or any other group or religion.

New Age— as humans have an astrological chart, so does the Earth and it moves though the different signs of the Zodiac, taking thousands of years to do so. Around the year 2,000CE the Earth moves from Pisces into Aquarius.

Occult—literally 'that which is hidden'; indicates unusual or specialist knowledge.

Pagan—from the Latin meaning 'one who lives in the countryside' and now used as an umbrella term for non-christains usually practising polytheistic, or nature based religions.

Path—a philosophical or magical grouping within the pagan community—also refers to an individual's philosophical or religious life-choices.

Sabbat—a generic name for a Witch festival.

Samhain—festival of year end and beginning held on 31st October, or the full moon nearest o this date; christianised as Hallowe'en.

Satanism—nothing to do with Witches or Witchcraft. It is some-times worship of Satan, sometimes the inversion of christianity, but *must* imply a belief in christianity.

Spell—a magical operation.

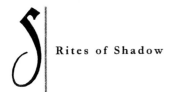

Spring Equinox—festival known as Eostra—christianised as 'Easter' - or Eostra.

Summer Solstice—midsummer festival also known as Litha.

Wicca—Anglo-Saxon word for Witch usually translated as meaning 'wise' or 'wisecraft'.

Widdershins—movements made in an anti-clock direction.

Wise One—respectful name for a Witch.

Witch—an adherent of the pre-christian religion of this Isle. Or one skilled in the magic associated with the pre-christian religion of this Isle.

Yule—midwinter festival held around the winter solstice.

The following titles by E. A. St George

The Thursden Correspondence
The Thaumateurgicon
Basic Magic Spells
Under Regulus
Book of Ghastly Curses
Songs of Sorcery
A Guide to the Gods of Ancient Egypt
The Theurgicon
Ancient & Modern Cat Worshop
Magical Purification
The Necronomicon
Spells of Laughter
Drugs & the Occult
A Pagan Book of the Dead
The Dream Tree
Zodiac in Gems
Notes on Magical Work
Legends of the Lizards
Oddball Prayer Book
'Dog is 'God' Spelt Backwards

are available from Raven.
Send SAE for full book list to:

RAVEN
17 Melton Fields
Brickyard Lane
North Ferriby
East Yorkshire HU13 3HE

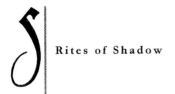

Other titles from ignotus press

Malleus Satani - The Hammer of Satan
Suzanne Ruthven
The inside story of the dark years of the satanic abuse myth that has now become a pagan classic. See how easily the public and Social Services were manipulated by misinformation and ignorance.
Paperback : 198pp : £9.95   ISBN 0 9522689-0-6

What You Call Time
A Guide to Witchcraft & Ritual Magic
Suzanne Ruthven
A conversation piece between practitioners of many occult traditions who reveal the inner secrets of the Paths. These are subjects normally only spoken about between initiates, making this a true guide to magic as it is worked in Britain today and pulls no punches in speaking the truth.
Paperback : 278pp : £9.95   ISBN 0 9522689-3-0

Liber Ægyptius—The Book of Egyptian Magic
Mélusine Draco
The most wide ranging and accessible book available on the practise of real Egyptian magic as taught by the Temple of Khem. This is a book for serious students who want to understand and practise a magic that is older than the pyramids.
Paperback : 240pp : £9.95 ISBN 0 9522689-4-9

The Hollow Tree—An Elementary Guide to the Qabalah
Mélusine Draco
An extremely through yet elementary guide to the use of and working with the Tarot and Qabalah. An excellent, practical introduction to the roots of real Western Occultism: if you don't know the difference between Yesod and Geburah, or where to stick your Supernal Triangle, this book explains it all in easy to follow language. **Revised edition currently in preparation.**

The Egyptian Books of Days
Mélusine Draco

A guide to the calendars of ancient Egypt and essential for those working in the Egyptian Mystery Tradition. Includes prayer and divination times for the lucky and unlucky days.

Paperback : 136pp : £9.95 : ISBN: 1 903768 00 4

Whittlewood
Suzanne Ruthven

A novel based on genuine occult practice which introduces a priestess of the calibre of Dion Fortune's Vivien LeFay
Morgan. Murder, psychic apparitions, a good dollop of sex, combined with accurate and intimate occult knowledge make this book hard to put down. So curl up in your circle of lamp light and shudder deliciously as the horror unfolds.

Paperback : 312pp : £8.99   ISBN 0 9522689-2-2

The Art of Coarse Witchcraft
Rupert & Gabrielle Percy

Fact or fiction? This a squint-eyed view of what passes for witchcraft in today's society. A delightful romp through the highways and byways of British paganism—and mind where you're putting your feet!

Available autumn 2001

Titles planned for 2001/2002
The Witch's Treasury of the Countryside—Draco/Harriss
The Witch's Treasure for Home & Garden—Sempers & Ruthven
The Thelemic Handbook—Mélusine Draco
The Witch's Treasury—Sempers & Ruthven
The High Rise Witch—Fiona Walker-Craven
Thirteen Moons—Fiona Walker-Craven
Star Child - Mélusine Draco
The Egyptian Books of Nights— Mélusine Draco
The Atum-Re Revival—Mélusine Draco

$\int$

ignotus press & Corvus Books